1990

THE
**INSTITUTIONAL
INVESTOR**
SERIES IN FINANCE

The Debt/Equity Choice

THE FINANCIAL MANAGEMENT ASSOCIATION SURVEY AND SYNTHESIS SERIES

This unique series provides corporate executives and professional investors with the practical tools vital for making sound financial decisions in today's competitive markets. Comprehensive and readable, each book in the series focuses on a relevant topic, integrating research with the day-to-day concerns of finance practitioners. Other books in this continuing series are:

The FMA Series is part of the larger Institutional Investor Series in Finance.

The costs of research and development that made the Financial Management Association Survey and Synthesis Series possible were underwritten in part by support provided to the Financial Management Association by United Airlines, the Federal Reserve Bank of Philadelphia, and Ameritech.

THE DEBT/EQUITY CHOICE

Ronald W. Masulis

BALLINGER PUBLISHING COMPANY
A Subsidiary of Harper & Row, Publishers, Inc.

International Standard Book Number: 0-88730-360-9
                                    0-88730-368-4 (pbk.)

Library of Congress Catalog Card Number: 88-22214

Printed in the United States of America

Library of Congress Cataloging-in-Publication Data

Masulis, Ronald W.

The debt/equity choice.

(The Institutional investor series in finance)
(The Financial Management Association survey and synthesis series)
Bibliography: p.
Includes index.
1. Corporations—Finance.   2. Corporations—Finance—Decision making.
3. Saving and investment.   Savings and investment—Decision making.
5. Stocks—Prices.   I. Title.   II. Series.   III. Series: Financial Management
Association survey and synthesis series.
HG4011.M28   1988   658.1'5   88-22214
ISBN 0-88730-360-9
ISBN 0-88730-368-4 (pbk.)
89 90 91 HC 6 5 4 3 2

Contents

Acknowledgments

I would like to thank the many colleagues who read drafts of this book, especially James Brickley, Thomas Copeland, Harry DeAngelo, Richard Green, Ronald Lease, Rodney Roenfeldt, Robert Taggart, Sheridan Titman, and Michael Vetsuypens, who made valuable comments. Of course, I am responsible for any remaining errors or omissions.

1

Leverage Ratios and Financing Decisions

The Empirical Evidence

The 1980s have witnessed substantial advances in the study of capital structure on both theoretical and empirical levels. This book surveys this body of work, emphasizing the empirical evidence, with the aim of stimulating further progress in this area. Although broad in coverage, this survey is not meant to be an exhaustive cataloguing of the capital structure literature. Instead, those articles containing more important evidence or promising methodological approaches are reviewed.[1]

Broadly interpreted, capital structure encompasses a corporation's (including its subsidiaries') publicly issued securities, private placements, bank debt, trade debt, leasing contracts, tax liabilities, pension liabilities, deferred compensation to management and employees, performance guarantees, product warranties, and other contingent liabilities. This list represents the major claims to a corporation's assets. Increases or reductions in any of these claims represents a form of capital structure change. The major focus of attention here is on how capital structure and its alteration affect the values of the firm and its various claims. However, given the nature of existing evidence, this survey emphasizes the valuation effects of changes in corporate securities and changes in firms' leverage ratios.[2]

One way to assess the importance of the capital structure is to look at the size of annual corporate security sales. In 1987, $152.0 billion in corporate debt and $62.0 billion in corporate equity securities were sold publicly in the United States, according to Securities Exchange Commission (SEC) statistics. At the same time, billions of dollars of debt and equity securities were being repurchased by U.S. corporations, indicating a conscious decision on the part of corporations to alter their existing capital structures. At the individual firm level, 1987 witnessed major capital structure changes by some of the best known U.S. corporations. For example, Occidental Petroleum sold 38 million shares of common stock raising over $1 billion, General Motors announced plans to buy back 60 million shares representing 20 percent of its outstanding common stock at a cost of over $4.7 billion, and Holiday Inns issued $900 million in subordinated debentures. What are the costs and benefits of these actions? How do security prices react to these announcements? What do these security price reactions tell us about the impact of capital structure change on firm value? What are the advantages of issuing various forms of debt and equity? How do firm characteristics differ across issuers of various types of liabilities? These are only a few of the questions to be addressed in this book.

Aggregate Sources of Financing, Aggregate Security Offerings, and Leverage Ratio Evidence

In studying firm leverage choices, it is useful to consider the alternative sources of capital available to firms over time. This review is especially relevant given that the major means of increasing equity capital is through reinvestment of firm profits rather than through the sale of new equity claims in the capital market. In this context, cash dividends clearly act like a stock repurchase in lowering equity capital in the firm while reinvestment of earnings adjusted for depreciation represents a *net* increase in equity capital.

Table 1–1 summarizes the internal as well as external sources of funds for nonfarm, nonfinancial corporations over the 1946–1986 period.[3] There are several noteworthy trends. The proportion of corporate funds obtained from undistributed profits, the major source of equity capital, has declined over this forty-year period.[4]

Table 1–1. Sources of Funds for Non-Farm, Non-Financial Corporate Business, 1946–1986

Year	Total Funds	Undistributed Profits		External Funds		Long-Term Debt[a]		Short-Term Debt		Other Fund Sources[b]	
1946	19.4	8.8	45%	10.6	55%	3.6	19%	3.3	17%	3.7	19%
1947	27.3	13.1	48%	14.2	52%	5.4	20%	3.0	11%	5.8	21%
1948	24.3	14.5	60%	9.8	40%	6.7	28%	−0.2	−1%	3.3	14%
1949	10.2	9.8	96%	0.4	4%	4.9	48%	−1.8	−18%	−2.7	−26%
1950	38.4	14.4	38%	24.0	63%	4.2	11%	3.9	10%	15.9	41%
1951	27.5	11.3	41%	16.2	59%	6.4	23%	4.1	15%	5.7	21%
1952	17.8	9.7	54%	8.1	46%	8.1	46%	1.5	8%	−1.5	−8%
1953	16.1	9.8	61%	6.3	39%	6.2	39%	−0.4	−2%	0.5	3%
1954	15.3	9.6	63%	5.7	37%	6.8	44%	−0.3	−2%	−0.8	−5%
1955	37.7	14.2	38%	23.5	62%	6.6	18%	3.8	10%	13.1	35%
1956	28.9	13.7	47%	15.2	53%	7.4	26%	5.3	18%	2.5	9%
1957	24.2	12.7	52%	11.5	48%	10.1	42%	1.8	7%	−0.4	−2%
1958	20.7	9.0	43%	11.7	57%	10.5	51%	0.0	0%	1.2	6%
1959	33.7	13.3	39%	20.4	61%	8.3	25%	4.2	12%	7.9	23%
1960	24.1	11.1	46%	13.0	54%	7.4	31%	4.4	18%	1.2	5%
1961	29.6	10.5	35%	19.1	65%	10.5	35%	1.7	6%	6.9	23%
1962	30.4	13.3	44%	17.1	56%	9.0	30%	3.5	12%	4.6	15%
1963	36.6	15.1	41%	21.5	59%	8.1	22%	3.9	11%	9.5	26%
1964	40.7	19.0	47%	21.7	53%	7.8	19%	5.9	14%	8.0	20%
1965	57.6	23.8	41%	33.8	59%	7.6	13%	11.4	20%	14.8	26%
1966	60.7	25.7	42%	35.0	58%	14.3	24%	9.5	16%	11.2	18%
1967	53.3	22.7	43%	30.6	57%	19.2	36%	8.1	15%	3.3	6%
1968	71.5	22.6	32%	48.9	68%	15.0	21%	13.0	18%	20.9	29%
1969	72.5	19.9	27%	52.6	73%	14.6	20%	19.2	26%	18.8	26%
1970	54.0	14.5	27%	39.5	73%	26.3	49%	7.9	15%	5.3	10%
1971	72.0	20.3	28%	51.7	72%	32.8	46%	4.3	6%	14.6	20%
1972	94.4	27.4	29%	67.0	71%	26.4	28%	17.4	18%	23.2	25%
1973	144.9	43.3	30%	101.6	70%	20.7	14%	36.9	25%	44.0	30%
1974	155.9	51.1	33%	104.8	67%	26.4	17%	43.9	28%	34.5	22%
1975	84.3	50.8	60%	33.5	40%	38.5	46%	−11.5	−14%	6.5	8%
1976	142.3	65.1	46%	77.2	54%	38.4	27%	16.7	12%	22.1	16%
1977	173.1	76.7	44%	96.4	56%	36.0	21%	36.1	21%	24.3	14%
1978	235.4	89.1	38%	146.3	62%	33.3	14%	51.8	22%	61.2	26%
1979	260.4	105.2	40%	155.2	60%	21.0	8%	66.9	26%	67.3	26%
1980	233.9	88.1	38%	145.8	62%	53.1	23%	39.5	17%	53.2	23%
1981	222.5	78.7	35%	143.8	65%	22.8	10%	71.7	32%	49.3	22%
1982	124.8	39.7	32%	85.1	68%	44.0	35%	36.4	29%	4.7	4%
1983	199.0	52.4	26%	145.6	73%	57.3	29%	31.3	16%	58.0	29%
1984	254.9	72.7	29%	182.2	71%	−7.5	−3%	129.0	51%	60.7	24%
1985	190.8	53.9	28%	136.9	72%	15.3	8%	69.9	37%	51.7	27%
1986	178.5	38.7	22%	139.8	78%	33.3	19%	76.1	43%	30.4	17%

a. New Issues of equity are included here in addition to corporate bonds and mortgages. However, equity represents a very minor portion of the capital raised from selling these long-term instruments.

b. Other fund sources consist of tax liabilities, trade debt, and direct foreign investment in the United States.

Source: President's Economic Report, January 1988, p. 354

At the same time short-term debt and trade debt plus direct foreign investment have increased as a proportion of total sources of capital. In recent years there have actually been significant *net* decreases in equity financing due to stock repurchases, takeovers, and "going-private" transactions. In a "going-private" transaction, the entire equity interest in a public corporation is purchased by a small group of investors that generally includes current management. These trends imply that the average corporate leverage ratio should be increasing, especially over the latter portion of this period.

Looking at the aggregate level of public sales of debt and equity securities by business firms over a more extensive period shows wide variability in the proportions of external financing represented by major types of security claims. Table 1–2 highlights these patterns by presenting annual SEC security offering statistics, broken down by major security classes.

Table 1–2. Business Securities Offered for Cash ($ millions)[a]

Year	Total Offerings	Type of Security					
		Common Stock[b]	Percent of Total	Preferred Stock	Percent of Total	Bonds and Notes	Percent of Total
1934	397	19	5	6	2	372	94
1939	2,164	87	4	98	5	1,979	91
1940	2,677	108	4	183	7	2,386	89
1941	2,667	110	4	167	6	2,389	90
1942	1,062	34	3	112	11	917	86
1943	1,170	56	5	124	11	990	85
1944	3,202	163	5	369	12	2,670	83
1945	6,011	397	7	758	13	4,855	81
1946	6,900	891	13	1,127	16	4,882	71
1947	6,577	779	12	762	12	5,036	77
1948	7,078	614	9	492	7	5,973	84
1949	6,052	736	12	425	7	4,890	81
1950	6,362	811	13	631	10	4,920	77
1951	7,741	1,212	16	838	11	5,691	74
1952	9,534	1,369	14	564	6	7,601	80
1953	8,898	1,326	15	489	5	7,083	80
1954	9,516	1,213	13	816	9	7,488	79
1955	10,240	2,185	21	635	6	7,420	72

Table 1–2. Business Securities Offered for Cash ($ millions)[a] (Cont.)

Year	Total Offerings	Type of Security					
		Common Stock[b]	Percent of Total	Preferred Stock	Percent of Total	Bonds and Notes	Percent of Total
1956	10,939	2,301	21	636	6	8,002	73
1957	12,884	2,516	20	411	3	9,957	77
1958	11,558	1,334	12	571	5	9,653	84
1959	9,748	2,027	21	531	5	7,190	74
1960	10,154	1,664	16	409	4	8,081	80
1961	13,165	3,294	25	450	3	9,420	72
1962	10,705	1,314	12	422	4	8,969	84
1963	12,211	1,011	8	343	3	10,856	89
1964	13,957	2,679	19	412	3	10,865	78
1965	14,782	1,473	10	724	5	12,585	85
1966	17,385	1,901	11	580	3	14,904	86
1967	24,014	1,927	8	881	4	21,206	88
1968	21,261	3,885	18	636	3	16,740	79
1969	25,997	7,640	29	691	3	17,666	68
1970	37,451	7,037	19	1,390	4	29,023	77
1971	43,229	9,485	22	3,683	9	30,061	70
1972	39,705	10,707	27	3,371	8	25,628	65
1973	31,680	7,642	24	3,341	11	20,700	65
1974	37,820	4,050	11	2,273	6	31,497	84
1975	53,632	7,414	14	3,459	6	42,759	80
1976	53,314	8,305	16	2,803	5	42,206	79
1977	54,229	8,047	15	3,916	7	42,266	78
1978	29,949	7,724	26	1,757	6	20,468	68
1979	37,248	8,816	24	1,964	5	26,468	71
1980	67,126	19,282	29	3,194	5	44,650	67
1981	65,888	25,226	38	1,696	3	38,966	59
1982	72,152	23,197	32	4,948	7	44,007	61
1983	102,620	45,153	44	7,615	7	49,852	49
1984	85,948	22,151	26	4,219	5	59,578	69
1985	131,508	36,480	28	6,457	5	88,571	68
1986	228,410	55,317	24	11,145	5	161,948	71
1987	216,990	56,169	26	8,811	4	152,010	70

a. Business securities offered include securities offered by corporate and noncorporate business enterprises such as limited partnerships. Beginning 1978 excludes private placements. These figures are gross proceeds unadjusted for flotation costs including underwriting fees.

b. Common stock combines the conventional ownership shares of corporate business and securities issued by noncorporate business, such as limited partnership interests, voting trust certificates, and condominium securities.

Source: U.S. Securities and Exchange Commission Monthly Statistical Review.

The table indicates that U.S. corporations consistently have issued larger dollar amounts of debt than equity, although debt varies from 94 percent all the way down to 49 percent of the dollar value of securities issued in the 1934–1987 period. Yet these figures greatly understate the proportion of the firm's outside financing represented by debt, since private placement debt, bank loans, and trade debt are all excluded from these figures. Table 1–2 indicates a much higher level of equity financing than Table 1–1, in part because (1) it includes regulated utilites, which have a high propensity to issue equity securities, (2) it does not net out stock repurchases, and (3) it includes sales of partnership units that in recent years make up nearly half of the common stock figure.

In a recent study of seasoned primary and primary-secondary equity financing by firms listed on the New York Stock Exchange (NYSE) and the American Stock Exchange (AMEX), Kalay and Shimrat report that equity offerings were made only infrequently over the 1970–1982 period.[5] On average, only about 3.65 percent of these firms sold equity in any given year and, excluding utilities, the frequency of equity offerings was only 1.92 percent per year. In short U.S. industrial firms rarely undertake equity offerings. A partial explanation for the dominance of debt in external financing is the fixed maturity characteristic of debt securities, which necessitates their periodic refinancing.

The flotation costs associated with security offerings to the public represent a significant fraction of gross proceeds from these sales. For underwritten stock offerings, these costs range from 13.74 percent for issues under $0.5 million in gross proceeds to 3.95 percent for issues exceeding $100 million, as documented in Smith, Eckbo and Masulis, and an earlier study by the SEC staff.[6] Titled the "Costs of Flotations of Registered Issues," the SEC studies also found smaller flotation costs for convertible debt issues and especially for nonconvertible debt issues. In the case of convertible debt, flotation costs range from 14.56 percent for issues under $1 million to 1.17 percent for issues over $100 million. In the case of nonconvertible debt, flotation costs range from 11.51 percent for small issues under $0.5 million to 0.83 percent for issues over $100 million. More interesting is the SEC finding that flotation costs of nonconvertible debt issues rise with a drop in debt rating class, even after taking into account issue size. This evidence taken as a whole sugggests that riskier securities have higher proportional flotation costs.

The significance of flotation costs may represent an important element in the capital structure decision. The previous evidence indicates that substantial scale economies in terms of flotation costs can be realized in security sales. One effect of these scale economies is to encourage less frequent but larger security offerings, yielding one motive for firms to be away from their optimum capital structures. The SEC studies indicate that sales of equity securities, with their generally higher risk levels, entail higher flotation costs than do offerings of debt securities. However, debt security issuance involves additional flotation costs at their refinancing dates, implying a benefit to long-term debt issues.

The most common description of a firm's capital structure is in terms of its financial leverage or debt to total asset ratio. When aggregated over all U.S industrial firms, this ratio tends to change slowly over time as documented by Holland and Myers and other studies.[7] The annual statistics of mean leverage ratios for U.S. industrial firms as reported by Holland and Myers are reproduced on Table 1–3.

Taggart studied this and other time series evidence on aggregate industrial leverage and aggregate financing decisions over this century.[8] He observes that substantial amounts of debt existed prior to the enactment of the U.S. corporate income tax with its interest tax deduction. He finds some interesting trends in the proportion of total corporate financings represented by long-term and short-term debt, namely that they have increased since 1945, and especially during the 1970s. Taggart suggests that these trends appear to be related to increases in corporate and personal tax rates, the expected inflation rate, and the decline in the relative size of government debt. As will be shown, these patterns are consistent with some of the recently developed theories of capital structure.

Table 1–3. Leverage Ratios of U.S. Corporations

Year	All U.S. Corporations			Manufacturing Corporations	
	Debt/ Total Assets	Long-Term Debt/ Long-Term Capital	Debt/ Total Assets	Long-Term Debt/ Long-Term Capital	Debt/ Total Assets
1926	—	.21	—	.09	—
1927	—	.22	—	.09	—
1928	—	.23	—	.10	—
1929	.13	.23	—	.09	—
1930	.18	.24	—	.10	—
1931	.25	.25	—	.10	—
1932	.39	.26	—	.11	—
1933	.37	.26	—	.10	—
1934	.32	.26	—	.10	—
1935	.36	.26	—	.10	—
1936	.24	.26	—	.10	—
1937	.27	.26	.53	.10	.26
1938	.41	.27	.54	.11	.25
1939	.32	.27	.55	.11	.25
1940	.33	.26	.57	.11	.27
1941	.38	.26	.58	.11	.31
1942	.44	.24	.61	.10	.35
1943	.28	.23	.63	.09	.36
1944	.28	.23	.64	.09	.34
1945	.25	.21	.65	.09	.30
1946	.16	.21	.64	.10	.30
1947	.17	.22	.63	.11	.31
1948	.17	.23	.62	.12	.32
1949	.23	.23	.62	.12	.28
1950	.18	.23	.63	.11	.31
1951	.19	.23	.63	.13	.35
1952	.21	.24	.65	.15	.36
1953	.21	.25	.65	.15	.36
1954	.22	.25	.65	.15	.34
1955	.16	.24	.66	.15	.35
1956	.15	.25	.65	.16	.36
1957	.17	.26	.65	.17	.38
1958	.17	.26	.65	.17	.37
1959	.16	.27	.66	.17	.38
1960	.18	.27	.66	.17	.38

Table 1–3. Leverage Ratios of U.S. Corporations (Continued)

Year	All U.S. Corporations			Manufacturing Corporations	
	Debt/ Total Assets	Long-Term Debt/ Long-Term Capital	Debt/ Total Assets	Long-Term Debt/ Long-Term Capital	Debt Total Assets
1961	.16	.28	.66	.18	.43
1962	.21	—	—	—	ّ—
1963	.18	.28	.68	.17	.38
1964	.17	.28	.68	.18	.39
1965	.17	.28	.69	.19	.40
1966	.22	.29	.69	.21	.43
1967	.19	.29	.69	.21	.42
1968	.18	.30	.70	.23	.45
1969	.22	.31	.70	.23	.45
1970	.27	.32	.71	.26	.49
1971	.26	.33	.72	.27	.69
1972	.24	.33	.72	.26	.49
1973	.31	.34	.73	.26	.51
1974	.38	.34	.74	.27	.53
1975	.32	.34	.74	.28	.52
1976	.32	.34	.74	.28	.53
1977	.34	.34	.74	.27	.53
1978	.35	.34	.75	.28	.54
1979	.36	.33	.74	.28	.55
1980	.32	.33	.74	.28	.56
1981	.29	.32	.73	.28	.56
1982	.29	.33	.73	.29	.56
1983	.26	.33	.74	.28	.57
1984	.27	.34	.74	.29	.57
1985	.30	—	—	—	—
1986	.31	—	—	—	—

Source: Robert A. Taggart, Jr., "Secular Patterns in the Financing of U.S. Corporations," in Benjamin M. Friedman, ed., *Corporate Capital Structures in the United States* (Chicago: Univesity of Chicago Press, 1985). All figures are in book value terms except for column 2 (Debt/Total Assets) which is an estimate of the leverage ratio using market value data. The original source for most of these figures is Daniel M. Holland and Stewart C. Myers, "Trends in Corporate Profitability and Capital Costs," in R. Lindsay, ed., *The Nation's Needs: Three Studies* (New York: Committee for Economic Development, 1979). Post-1980 data was obtained directly from Robert Taggart and from the Statistics of Income, Corporation Returns, Table 2.

Flotation Cost Differences and the Financing Choice

The observation that equity offerings have larger flotation costs than debt offerings potentially has implications for the firm's capital structure decisions, since it follows that internal funds are cheaper than external funds and that equity securities are more expensive to sell than debt securities (especially long-term debt, where refinancing costs are incurred infrequently). Managerial preferences in raising funds appear to reflect these cost differences, as reported by Donaldson.[9] However, other explanations also are consistent with this set of managerial preferences, as will be shown.

The importance of flotation costs appears to have changed with the implementation of shelf registration and the heightened level of investment banking competition to underwrite these issues. Two empirical studies, Kidwell, Marr, and Thompson and Bhagat, Marr, and Thompson, find that under shelf registration, underwriting costs have dropped significantly (on average, 0.3 percent of gross proceeds for debt offerings and 1 percent for equity offerings) without any offsetting increase in the other costs of flotation.[10] With this lowering in the overall costs of selling both debt and equity securities (on a percentage basis), and with the expansion of other low-cost avenues for raising external funds such as commercial paper, changes in the size, timing, and form of firms' capital structure decisions should be observed if flotation costs are indeed important to these decisions. Changes in capital structure decisions are especially likely if the flotation costs of debt relative to equity have changed. However, these speculations have yet to be tested.

Another important question related to flotation costs and firm financial policy has generated considerable interest. Smith presented evidence from a large sample of equity offerings that the flotation costs associated with rights offerings are substantially lower than those for underwritten offerings, even after taking into account differences in size.[11] Yet, over 95 percent of all seasoned equity offerings in the United States in recent years have used a firm commitment underwriting contract. Later studies by Bhagat and by Smith and Dhatt have developed additional evidence which seems to support the conclusion that underwritten offerings are more costly, while Hansen and Pinkerton present evidence that ownership structure also can have a bearing on these differences in flotation costs.[12] In a 1987 paper, Hansen adds to this puzzle by presenting evidence that standby rights offerings are considerably less costly than firm commitment underwritings and yet standby offerings also are infrequently used.[13] Eckbo and Masulis have analyzed the stock announcement effects and the flotation costs of a large sample of rights and underwritten offerings.[14] They find that for industrial issuers, stocks exhibit a small negative average return on the announcement of pure rights offerings that is less than offering flotation costs measured as a percent of the market value of these stocks. In contrast, stocks exhibit negative average returns on the announcement of firm commitment and standby offerings that substantially exceed offering flotation costs as a percent of the market value of these stocks. Thus, the two offering methods employing underwriters have negative announcement effects that cannot be attributed solely to the negative valuation effects of flotation costs, while the pure rights offering sample exhibits no such negative valuation effect.

Evidence on the Timing and Predictability of Financing Decisions

Flotation cost is closely related to the frequency and timing of security offerings. Several studies have uncovered evidence relevant to this issue. Most notable is a 1986 study by Mikkelson and Partch, who examined the frequencies of security offerings as well as originations of bank debt, and sales of private placements for a sample of 360 NYSE- and AMEX-listed firms over a ten-year period.[15] They report finding 299 initial announcements of public offerings of securities and 296 announcements of credit agreements, term loans, and private placement of debt. This implies a surprisingly small frequency of public or private external financing announcements. Their findings also indicate that raising external funds by bank loan or private placement of debt occurs 50 percent more frequently than public offerings of debt, although the size of the latter is likely to be larger.[16] This evidence suggests that the effects of bank debt and private placements of securities deserve more extensive study.

If firms have optimal capital structures that are relatively stable over time, then security issues should exhibit a certain degree of predictability. Taggart's study of changes in long-term debt and equity by U.S. nonfinancial corporations indicates that firms make capital structure decisions with a long-term target leverage ratio in mind.[17] The data also seem to indicate that firms prefer to issue equity when the stock's price is relatively high.

Corroboration for these conclusions is found in Scott and Johnson's survey of chief financial officers of the Fortune 1000 corporations.[18] Eighty-nine percent of respondents indicated that they use some measure of leverage in arriving at their firm's debt/equity choice. Of these executives, 92 percent indicated a preference for a book-value measure of leverage. They also reported that their primary measures of leverage are long-term debt to total capitalization and the times-interest-earned ratio (operating income divided by annual interest payments). Over half of these executives stated that industry-wide ratios were also an important influence on their decisions. Last, 64 percent of these respondents stated a preference for target leverage ratios in the 20–40 percent range.

Studying the debt/equity choice of British firms Marsh found that this choice can be predicted partially by the current proportions of the firm's short-term and long-term debt and level of earnings retention relative to their historical levels.[19] He reports that the timing of a firm's security issuance tends toward periods when the equity market in general and the firm's stock in particular are experiencing large price gains and when interest rates are at relatively low levels. This pattern may reflect the effects of lower market discount rates increasing firm values at the same time that more investment projects become profitable. Marsh also observes that "smaller firms, those with few fixed assets, and those with greater bankruptcy risk are more likely to issue equity." Reinforcing this earlier evidence, Asquith and Mullins, and Masulis, and Korwar have reported evidence that seasoned equity offerings can be predicted in part from prior stock price gains for these firms and prior gains by stock market indexes.[20]

2

Capital Structure Change and Its Relation to Firm Value

Some of the most interesting recent findings in the corporate finance literature concern the financial implications of capital structure decisions for the firm and its common stock. But before turning to the evidence, a basic introduction to the methodology commonly used in analyzing security price reactions to capital structure changes is called for. Security returns play an important role since, in an informationally efficient capital market, security prices immediately capitalize the economic significance of announced capital structure changes. As a result, security price responses to corporate announcements offer important evidence of the market's consensus beliefs on the valuation consequences of these decisions. However, security prices also can change in response to various macroeconomic developments and to changes in market risk premiums. Thus, to isolate a firm-specific announcement effect, a security return must be adjusted for both contemporaneous marketwide movements and the security's normal rate of return.

Methodological Review

Two methodologies are commonly used for analyzing security price data: event study analysis and multivariate regression. In a typical event study, a sample of firms making a particular type of corporate announcement, called the event, is analyzed. Then, for each firm, a time series of daily security returns centered around its specific announcement date is collected. This procedure is repeated for each firm making a similar type of announcement, even though these announcements generally occur on different calendar dates. The time series of daily returns are then labeled in "event time" according to the number of trading days by which the return precedes or follows that security's announcement date. By convention the announcement date is defined as event date zero. For each event date, the associated daily return for each security in the sample is averaged, and this procedure is repeated for all event dates, to create a single time series of event date average returns. The announcement mean return can be compared statistically with the average returns over the remaining event dates to assess the significance of the typical announcement effect.

The major limitation of this methodology is that it does not adjust for the varying extent of prior market anticipation of these announcements, which affects the magnitude of the associated security price reactions. A second limitation is that occasionally a firm's initial announcement of an event can (1) be vague as to the specific details and (2) indicate that an event is likely but not certain. As a result, the valuation impact of the event will be spread over the initial and one or more follow-up announcement dates. Last, if the firm's event is especially predictable, for example, because the firm tends to repeat the event periodically, then much of the valuation effect due to the event will be capitalized in the stock price prior to the announcement.

Multiple regression analysis is used frequently in two corporate finance contexts. It is used to estimate the marginal relationships between individual security announcement returns and a set of explanatory variables describing the information contained in each firm's announcement. That is to say, this technique measures the relationship between announcement returns and one explanatory variable after the effects of all the other explanatory variables have been extracted. This statistical technique also is used to estimate the incremental relationships between leverage ratios and other firm characteristics from a large cross-section of firms.

One advantage of multiple regression analysis is that it can separate out the joint effects of several explanatory variables. It also is subject, however, to certain limitations in the face of explanatory variables measured with error (proxy variables) and the unavailability of data on the market value of firm debt, which makes measurement of leverage ratios difficult. Having noted some of the major limitations of the data and the statistical techniques, we turn now to the evidence.

Summary of Recent Empirical Evidence

In the last few years a vast body of evidence has been amassed concerning market reaction to corporate investment, financing, and dividend decisions. Table 2–1 presents a summary of average stock price reactions to various capital structure change announcements. The studies are noteworthy for their large samples of corporate announcements and their use of daily closing prices of common stocks. On the surface, the evidence on stock market reactions to security offering announcements is paradoxical. Announcements of security offerings consistently are greeted with nonpositive stock price response, even though these corporate decisions are voluntary and presumably are associated with profitable investment projects. What is more puzzling, when stocks or convertible securities are issued, the average stock price reaction is actually significantly negative, and largest in the case of common stock offerings.[1] Further, when common stock is issued, there is a small negative announcement return of 3.3 percent, but when the opposite capital structure change is announced—namely, a tender offer to repurchase stock (which on average involves a similar percentage change in stock)—there is a large announcement return of 16.4 percent. A greater predictability of equity offerings is also an unlikely explanation, given their rarity.

Table 2–1 highlights some other interesting patterns of evidence in these various studies. In almost every case where a statistically significant announcement effect is observed, it is consistent in sign with the direction of the change in firm leverage.[2] This pattern is especially clear if one interprets convertible debt issuance as a delayed issue of equity and recognizes that private placement debt can have equity "kickers" that make it much like a convertible issue.[3]

Table 2-1. Average Stock Price Reactions to Leverage Change Announcements for U.S. Firms

Study	Type of Announcement	Sample Size	Two-Day Mean Ann. Ret. (%)
	Leverage Increasing Decisions		
Masulis[a]	Exchange offers of debt for common stock	52	14.0 +*
Masulis[a]	Exchange offers of debt for preferred stock	24	3.53 +*
Pinegar and Lease[b]	Exchange offers of preferred for common stock	15	8.1*
Masulis[a]	Exchange offers of preferred for common stock	9	8.3 +*
McConnell and Schlarbaum[c]	Exchange offers of income bonds for preferred stock	24	2.2*
Masulis[d]	Repurchase of common stock by tender offer	199	16.4*
Masulis[d]	Debt-financed repurchase of common stock by tender offer	45	21.9*
Dann[e]	Repurchase of common stock by tender offer	142	15.4*
Vermaelen[f]	Repurchase of common stock by tender offer	131	14.1*
Vermaelen[f]	Secondary market repurchases of common stock	243	3.4*
DeAngelo, DeAngelo, & Rice[g]	"Going-private" transactions	72	28.3*
Linn and Pinegar[h]	Public offerings of nonconvertible preferred stock	294	.8
Dann and Mikkelson[i]	Public offerings of nonconvertible debt	150	-.4
Mikkelson and Partch[j]	Public offerings of nonconvertible debt (IND)	171	-.2
Eckbo[k]	Public offerings of nonconvertible nonmortgage debt	459	-.1
Eckbo[k]	Public offerings of nonconvertible mortgage debt	189	-.2
Mikkelson and Partch[j]	Private placement of debt (IND)	80	-.6
Mikkelson and Partch[j]	Bank debt borrowings (IND)	61	-.2
Mikkelson and Partch[j]	Initiation of credit agreements (IND)	155	.9*
Officer and Smith[l]	Withdrawal of common stock offering	31	2.4*

Table 2-1. Average Stock Price Reactions to Leverage Change Announcements for U.S. Firms (Continued)

Study	Type of Announcement	Sample Size	Two-Day Mean Ann. Ret. (%)
	Leverage Decreasing Decisions		
Masulis[a]	Exchange offers of common stock for debt	20	-9.9+*
Masulis[a]	Exchange offers of common for preferred stock	30	-2.6+*
Pinegar and Lease[b]	Exchange offers of common for preferred stock	30	-1.5*
Masulis[a]	Exchange offers of preferred stock for debt	9	-7.7+*
Finnerty[m]	Private swaps of common stock for debt	113	-1.1*
Peavy and Scott[n]	Private swaps of common stock for debt	93	-.6*
Rogers and Owers[o]	Private swaps of common stock for debt with no new debt issued	74	-1.1*
Rogers and Owers[o]	Private swaps of common stock for debt with new debt issued	34	-.9*
Asquith and Mullins[p]	Public offerings of common stock (IND)	128	-3.0*
Masulis and Korwar[q]	Public offerings of common stock (IND)	388	-3.3*
Masulis and Korwar[q]	Public offerings of common stock (IND) used to redeem debt	55	-3.8*
Mikkelson and Partch[j]	Public offerings of common stock (IND)	80	-3.6*
Kalay and Shimrat[r]	Public offerings of common stock (IND)	455	-3.4*
White and Luzstig[s]	Rights offerings of common stock	90	-1.0+*
Eckbo and Masulis[t]	Rights offerings of common stock (IND)	43	-1.7*
Eckbo and Masulis[t]	Standby offerings of common stock (IND)	39	-1.1*
Vora and Yoon[u]	Private placements of common stock	28	1.2
Wruck[v]	Private placements of common stock	99	1.1*
Dann and Mikkelson[i]	Rights offerings of convertible debt	38	-1.2*
Dann and Mikkelson[i]	Public offerings of convertible debt	132	-2.3*

17

Table 2-1. Average Stock Price Reactions to Leverage Change Announcements for U.S. Firms

Study	Type of Announcement	Sample Size	Two-Day Mean Ann. Ret. (%)
	Leverage Decreasing Decisions		
Masulis[a]	Exchange offers of debt for common stock	52	14.0 +*
Masulis[a]	Exchange offers of debt for preferred stock	24	3.53+*
Pinegar and Lease[b]	Exchange offers of preferred for common stock	15	8.1*
Masulis[a]	Exchange offers of preferred for common stock	9	8.3+*
McConnell and Schlarbaum[c]	Exchange offers of income bonds for preferred stock	24	2.2*
Masulis[d]	Repurchase of common stock by tender offer	199	16.4*
Masulis[d]	Debt-financed repurchase of common stock by tender offer	45	21.9*
Dann[e]	Repurchase of common stock by tender offer	142	15.4*
Vermaelen[f]	Repurchase of common stock by tender offer	131	14.1*
Vermaelen[f]	Secondary market repurchases of common stock	243	3.4*
DeAngelo, DeAngelo, & Rice[g]	"Going-private" transactions	72	28.3*
Linn and Pinegar[h]	Public offerings of nonconvertible preferred stock	294	.8
Dann and Mikkelson[i]	Public offerings of nonconvertible debt	150	-.4
Mikkelson and Partch[j]	Public offerings of nonconvertible debt (IND)	171	-.2
Eckbo[k]	Public offerings of nonconvertible nonmortgage debt	459	-.1
Eckbo[k]	Public offerings of nonconvertible mortgage debt	189	-.2
Mikkelson and Partch[j]	Private placement of debt (IND)	80	-.6
Mikkelson and Partch[j]	Bank debt borrowings (IND)	61	-.2
Mikkelson and Partch[j]	Initiation of credit agreements (IND)	155	.9*
Officer and Smith[l]	Withdrawal of common stock offering	31	2.4*

Table 2–1. Average Stock Price Reactions to Leverage Change Announcements for U.S. Firms (Continued)

e. Larry Dann, "Common Stock Repurchases: An Analysis of Returns to Bondholders and Stockholders," *Journal of Financial Economics 9* (1981): 113–38.

f. Theo Vermaelen, "Common Stock Repurchases and Market Signalling," *Journal of Financial Economics* (1981): 139–83.

g. Harry DeAngelo, Linda DeAngelo, and Edward M. Rice, "Going Private: Minority Freezeouts and Shareholder Wealth," *Journal of Law and Economics 27* (1984): 367–401.

h. Scott C. Linn and J. Michael Pinegar, "The Effect of Issuing Preferred Stock on Common and Preferred Stockholder Wealth," University of Iowa Working Paper, 1985.

i. Larry Dann and Wayne H. Mikkelson, "Convertible Debt Issuance, Capital Structure Change and Financing-Related Information: Some New Evidence," *Journal of Financial Economics 13* (1984): 157–86.

j. Wayne Mikkelson and Megan Partch, "Stock Price Effects and Costs of Secondary Distributions," *Journal of Financial Economics 14* (1985): 165–94.

l. Dennis Officer and Richard Smith, "Announcements of Withdrawn Security Offerings: Evidence on the Wealth Redistribution Hypothesis," *Journal of Financial Research 9* (1986): 229–38.

m. John D. Finnerty, "Stock-for-Debt Swaps and Shareholder Returns," *Financial Management 14* (1985) 5–17.

n. John W. Peavy and Jonathan A. Scott, "The Effect of Stock-for-Debt Swaps on Security Returns," *Financial Review 20* (1985): 303–27.

o. Ronald C. Rogers and James E. Owers, "Equity for Debt Exchanges and Stockholder Wealth," *Financial Management 14* (1985): 18–26.

p. Paul Asquith and David W. Mullins, "Equity Issues and Stock Price Dilution," *Journal of Financial Economics 15* (1986): 61–89.

q. Ronald W. Masulis and Ashok W. Korwar, "Seasoned Equity Offerings: An Empirical Investigation," *Journal of Financial Economics 15* (1986): 91–118.

r. Avner Kalay and Adam Shimrat, "Firm Value and Seasoned Equity Issues: Price Pressure, Wealth Redistribution or Negative Information," New York University Working Paper, 1985.

s. Robert W. White and Peter A. Lusztig, "The Price Effects of Rights Offerings," *Journal of Financial and Quantitative Analysis 15* (1980): 25–40.

t. Espen Eckbo and Ronald W. Masulis, "Rights vs. Underwritten Stock Offerings: An Empirical Analysis," Southern Methodist University Working Paper, 1987.

u. Gautam Vora and Seung Jin Yoon, "Price Impact of Private Placement of Common Stocks: A Signalling Approach to Capital Market Efficiency," Pennsylvania State University Working Paper, 1986.

v. Karen Wruck, "Private Equity Financing," unpublished Ph.D. dissertation, University of Rochester, 1987.

w. Vahan Janjigian, "The Leverage Changing Consequences of Convertible Debt Financing," *Financial Management* (Autumn 1987): 15–21.

x. Wayne Mikkelson, "Convertible Calls and Security Returns," *Journal of Financial Economics 9* (1981): 237–64.

This basic conclusion is reinforced if a greater weight is given to studies of approximately pure capital structure changes, events that involve no cash inflow to or outflow from the firm. Studies of these events have the advantage of avoiding the contaminating effects of simultaneous changes in firm asset structure that cash inflow and outflow induce. The major studies of pure capital structure changes have dealt with issuer exchange offers,[4] debt-financed issuer tender offers of stock,[5] issuer exchange offers involving income bonds,[6] conversion-forcing calls of convertible bonds,[7] and common stock offerings used to redeem debt.[8] These studies consistently report average stock price reactions of the same sign as the change in leverage as seen in Table 2–1. The current explanation for these various results and the corroborative evidence are reviewed in this book.

The various patterns of stock price reactions to capital structure changes provide a useful initial perspective on the capital market's assessment of specific corporate financial decisions. The evidence supports corporate finance theories positing capital structure relevance for stock price as well as firm value. These theories presume that the basic features of the corporate environment such as (1) the corporate and personal tax code, (2) bankruptcy procedures and their cost, (3) contract law and the costs of contract design, monitoring, and enforcement, (4) managerial compensation systems, (5) the distribution of ownership and voting rights, (6) flotation costs, and (7) government regulation influence the firm's capital structure decisions. Interpreting the market reaction to these capital structure decisions is complicated by the fact that investors are cognizant of management's access to better information on firm earnings prospects. Given the current structure of management incentives, a change in firm financial policy is likely to reflect changes in a firm's underlying earnings prospects which are known to management and can be inferred by the market. Thus, market reactions to these announcements are likely to incorporate both a direct effect of a financial policy change and an indirect information effect.[9]

The body of evidence presented on Table 2–1 raises an important question. If firms generally adjust their leverage ratios toward their optimum levels, why do stock prices react negatively to announcements of leverage decreases? One explanation for this phenomenon is that most firms operate below their optimum leverage ratios because of managerial risk aversion, a possible manifestation of the manager-stockholder agency problem (see Chapter 6). Currently, many researchers believe the explanation is due to some form of information effect positively related to the leverage change that dominate these price reactions. (This view will be discussed more fully in Chapter 7.)

If capital structure decisions are influenced by factors such as the corporate tax code and bankruptcy costs, then firms coming from the same industry, which have similar tax benefits and financial distress probabilities and cost functions, should exhibit capital structures that are more closely related than firms in general. This observation has motivated a number of studies of industry capital structure patterns. The most notable of these recent studies are by Bowen, Daley and Huber, Castanias, and Bradley, Jarrell, and Kim.[10] In each of these studies, more variation was found in mean leverage ratios across industries than in firm leverage ratios within industries. These studies also uncovered some other interesting patterns across industries. Bowen, Daley, and Huber found that industries with higher tax shields (such as special depreciation or depletion allowances) relative to total revenue, were found to exhibit lower leverage ratios.[11] Castanias found that industry bankruptcy probabilities are stable over time and that firms in industries with higher rates of bankruptcy have lower leverage ratios.[12] The patterns found in these studies are consistent with corporate taxes and bankruptcy costs having significant influences on the capital structure decision.

More direct evidence was found in a study by Campbell, testing the joint hypotheses that optimal capital structures exist for firms and that at least some major determinants of these optimum leverage ratios are industry related.[13] Classifying firms into two- and three-digit Standard Industrial Code (SIC) categories, Campbell reports that industry differences in firm leverage ratios (measured over five-year periods) are statistically significant. She also finds that industry leverage ratios change over time, as does the dispersion of firm leverage ratios within industries. However, the relative rankings of these two variables over time are significantly positively correlated for individual industries. These relationships are all consistent with the study's stated joint hypotheses.

Campbell then regresses firm leverage change, and leverage change adjusted for whether the firm is moving toward or away from the industry's leverage ratio, against the firm's stock return at the announcement of two relatively pure capital structure changes: forced exercise of convertible debt and debt-for-equity swaps. She finds evidence that the stock price reactions are significantly affected by whether the firm is moving toward the industry norm (positive reaction) or away from it (negative reaction). Campbell observes that this evidence supports the prediction that firms' optimal capital structures are at least partially related to industry-wide determinants.

While the previous evidence is suggestive of the importance of the capital structure decision, a more careful analysis is necessary before one can begin to understand the relationship between capital structure and firm value.[14] This linkage requires some knowledge of capital structure theories and their testable predictions. What makes this endeavor challenging is that many of the theories are complementary and thus their predictions are often similar. In the following chapters, these competing theories are categorized by their emphases on major determinants of capital structure change.

3

Tax Effects of
Capital Structure

A Theoretical Summary

One of the consistent themes in the corporate finance literature is the importance of tax considerations for capital structure decisions. This issue involves not only the effect of the corporate tax deductibility of debt but also the tax implications of these decisions for a firm's security holders. In these models debt securities are recognized to be more heavily taxed at the personal level than equity securities. Thus, even though debt issuance produces a corporate tax advantage, it also produces a personal tax disadvantage that varies across investors depending on their personal tax rates. This personal tax disadvantage directly affects the firm through a price discount on the sale of its more heavily taxed debt securities. Furthermore, investors will have differing preferences for debt and equity securities depending on their tax brackets. As a consequence, as firms in the aggregate issue additional debt, investors currently preferring equity must be enticed to switch to debt through larger and larger price discounts. The result is a diminished net tax advantage of debt. This conclusion is by itself important, because it implies that if any incremental costs of debt such as bankruptcy costs exist, they need not be large to offset the net tax advantage of debt. This issue will be considered further in the next section.

Miller argues that the net tax advantage of debt will be eliminated because firms will continue to issue debt as long as the net tax advantage is positive, presuming that bankruptcy costs are small enough to be safely ignored.[1] In this case there will be no capital structure effect on firm value. DeAngelo and Masulis observe that, with the existence of nondebt tax shields, such as depreciation, depletion allowances, investment, and foreign tax credits, firms will be uncertain as to whether or not they can fully utilize their debt tax deductions.[2] This observation implies that, if excess tax shields are costly to transfer, each firm will have an optimal tax-induced debt level where the expected net tax advantage of debt is exhausted. Thus, firms with large nondebt tax shields relative to expected earnings before interest and taxes are predicted to employ relatively less debt, everything else being the same.[3] The analysis also indicated that as nondebt tax shields divided by expected earnings changes, an opposite directional change in leverage should be observed. In this case, leverage changes affect firm values positively if the changes move the firms closer to their current optimum debt/equity ratios.

Under an optimal debt tax shield policy, a leverage decrease implies that a firm's management expects to utilize a smaller tax shield fully, which in most cases means lower expected earnings.[4] Thus, the leverage decline announcement is negative information about firm earnings, which should decrease the firm's stock price by more than the positive net effect of the debt adjustment. By the same logic, a leverage increase should cause a larger stock price gain because the two effects are reinforcing. This information argument also is consistent with the predictions of the earlier leverage signaling model of Ross.[5]

Several recent extensions of the earlier analysis of tax effects are especially noteworthy. Auerbach and King explore the conditions under which the leverage decision continues to be irrelevant when investors are forced to trade off the benefits of portfolio specialization for tax minimization with the costs of lost portfolio diversification.[6] Green and Talmor show that the cost of having excess tax shields creates incentives for a firm to lower its overall risk so as to decrease uncertainty over utilization of its tax shields.[7] One can interpret this result as saying that higher operating risk increases expected leverage costs, defined as the expected loss from unused tax shields. Mayer extends the DeAngelo-Masulis analysis by developing a multiperiod model that simultaneously determines a firm's optimal debt and investment decisions.[8] He focuses on the British tax system and emphasizes the effects of these decisions on a firm's cost of capital.[9] Ross considers the effects of a progressive personal tax structure and the firm's market risk (for example, its beta) on the firm's optimal leverage decision.[10] With a progressive tax structure, security holders' returns are taxed more heavily when the economy is doing well, and so in these states of the world, investors value equity income more highly than debt income due to equity's lower tax liability. Thus, firms with earnings that have a high correlation with the economy (that is, a high beta) are predicted to employ relatively more equity and less debt.[11]

Evidence on the Tax Implications of Capital Structure

Given the U.S. tax code's history of treating debt more favorably than corporate equity, capital structure changes are predicted to have tax-induced firm valuation effects under a number of existing theories. However, if firms have optimum leverage ratios that they attempt to reach, then movements to increase or decrease leverage should have positive valuation effects. This fact makes it difficult to draw conclusions about the effects of taxes from *average* stock price reactions to announced capital structure changes. An alternative approach for measuring tax effects is followed in two recent studies of approximately pure capital structure changes, by Masulis and by Mikkelson. Both authors studied the cross-sectional relationships between individual stock announcement returns and their measures of capital structure change.[12]

Masulis analyzed stock price reactions to issuer exchange offers and recapitalizations involving increases or decreases in firms' major classes of securities (common stock, preferred stock, and debt). More than half the cross-sectional variation in stock announcement returns was explained by changes in outstanding debt and percentage changes in leverage weighted by the market values of outstanding senior securities. Masulis argues that the leverage change variables capture the effects of wealth redistribution across senior security classes. Leverage changes were found to exhibit a significant positive relation with stock price, while a change in outstanding debt, which was segmented into positive and negative changes, was associated with an increase in stock price regardless of sign. This evidence is consistent with theories positing that leverage change is a signal of a like change in a firm's future earnings and that an adjustment of debt (in either direction) toward its optimum level has a positive effect on firm value. Using linear regression estimation, Mikkelson also found evidence of a significant positive relationship between stock returns on the announcement of calls of convertible debt and the size of the change in debt tax shields.

Yawitz and Anderson as well as Marshall and Yawitz argue that the U.S. tax code also affects the characteristics of corporate debt issues.[13] They note that, in general, corporations realize a net tax benefit from calling their debt issues early because the call premium is a tax-deductible expense to the issuer but prior to 1987 involved a lower capital gains tax liability to the tendering bondholder. Hence, even if bondholders have tax rates as high as the corporate rate, there is a net tax savings to the two parties from calling the debt. Boyce and Kalotay make a similar observation, noting that call features have negative price impacts for U.S. government and municipal bonds since the net tax advantage to the two parties is negative when the issuers are tax exempt.[14] This observation is consistent with the fact that calls are an extremely prevalent feature of corporate debt issues in the United States but not of federal government or municipal debt issues. A question that has not yet been answered is whether call features are prevalent in other countries with different tax structures.

An important element in several optimal capital structure models is the existence of excess corporate tax shields. Several recent studies have developed evidence on the proportion of corporations paying taxes in a given year. Cordes and Sheffrin estimate the distribution of expected marginal corporate tax rates on interest deductions for a U.S. Treasury Department sample of corporation tax records.[15] They conclude that only 56 percent of corporate receipts accrued to firms paying the maximum corporate tax rate on marginal earnings. Altshuler and Auerbach study the importance of restrictions on the use of tax credits and the inability to obtain refunds for tax losses.[16] Their findings suggest that the incidence of unused tax shields increased substantially in the early

1980s. Mayer cites evidence that, for the early 1980 period, only 40 percent of British companies were paying taxes on marginal profits.[17] Furthermore, in this same period tax loss carryforwards were nearly three times as large as the annual British corporate tax receipts. Mintz reports that only 50 percent of investment by Canadian manufacturing firms was undertaken by firms paying corporate taxes in the 1979–1981 period and that the incidence of firms with loss carryforwards is much higher in certain industries, such as mining.[18] Overall, the evidence suggests that the likelihood of excess corporate tax shields is significant.

Auerbach and Poterba extend the earlier analysis by studying the tax carryforward position of a sample of large industrial firms in the United States over the 1981–1984 period.[19] A firm's carryforward position is particularly interesting, because tax carryback opportunities presumably have been exhausted, and thus some loss of excess tax shield must be occurring. Auerbach and Poterba report that about 15 percent of their sampled firms had carryforwards. However, when weighted by asset holdings, only 6 percent of these corporate assets were associated with firms with carryforwards. This evidence indicates that it is primarily smaller firms that experience excess tax shields, although in certain industries such as airlines, automobile manufacture, oil, and steel the frequency of carryforwards ranges from 25 percent to over 40 percent. Auerbach and Poterba also report that positive carryforward positions tend to continue for a number of years. While this evidence seems to indicate that excess tax shields occur for a small portion of corporations, they noted that they were unable to measure the effects of excess investment tax credits or foreign tax credits, which can have an important bearing on the extent of a corporation's true level of excess tax shields, and that accounting data they were using was seriously understating the extent of loss carryforwards.

It is well known that financial leases enable the borrower (the lessee) to transfer to the lender (the lessor) those tax benefits associated with capital equipment depreciation and investment tax credits that otherwise would go to the borrower using a loan to finance a capital equipment purchase. Leasing can be mutually beneficial if the lessor is in a higher tax bracket than the lessee, as is the case if the lessee is experiencing losses, is tax exempt, or has excess tax shields, so that it is effectively in a zero tax bracket while the lessor is paying taxes. In this case, the lessee effectively can "sell" the excess tax deduction and investment tax credit associated with the leased equipment to the lessor for a reduction in the leasing payments. However, clear evidence that financial leases are frequently used for this purpose is surprisingly hard to find. A study of the tax status of lessors and lessees would certainly be quite useful.

In a recent study, Marston and Harris report evidence that debt and leases are close substitutes based on a large sample of U.S. firms' leasing and debt financing decisions over a recent six-year period.[20] However, on average, as reductions in nonlease debt are offset by increases in leases, it is on less than a dollar-for-dollar basis.[21]

Major revisions in national tax codes provide informative experiments for further analyzing the effects of taxes on corporate financial policy.[22] The major tax reform act of 1986 should be especially valuable to future researchers, but it also highlights the fact that basing decisions on a tax code presumed to exist in the future is a risky proposition as well.

Several studies of less dramatic tax changes are worth noting. When the U.S. tax code was changed in 1980 and 1981, corporate financial policy reacted very clearly. With the passage of the Bankruptcy Tax Act of 1980, early redemption of discount debt became taxable unless it was redeemed as part of a debt/equity swap with an independent investor. Substantial swap activity arose almost immediately, as documented by Finnerty and by Rogers and Owers, and ended abruptly with the enactment of the Tax Reform Act of 1984, which eliminated the tax benefits of this activity.[23]

Another important change in the tax law was the enactment of the Economic Recovery Tax Act of 1981, which made corporate leasing for the purpose of transferring excess tax shields less costly; this activity is commonly known as "safe harbor" leasing. Thus, it is not surprising that with the passage of this law substantial increases in corporate leasing activity were recorded over the year and a half that the law was in force.[24] Interestingly, over this period Stickney, Weil, and Wolfson report evidence that sales of excess tax shields occurred at substantial discounts.[25] So, even with the benefit of safe harbor leasing, only a portion of the value of these excess tax shields was captured by selling firms (particularly after broker costs are recognized).

In a study of a foreign tax law change, Vantheinen and Vermaelen report the effects of a major change in the corporate tax code in Belgium (a nation with a tax system similar in structure to this country's) on both corporate leverage decisions and stock price reactions to equity offerings.[26] They found that when a portion of the dividends from new equity capital were made deductible from corporate taxes, leverage ratios fell substantially. After the enactment of this tax code revision, the authors found that stock prices reacted positively to subsequent announcements of equity offerings, in stark contrast to what happens in the United States, where equity capital is not tax-deductible. In all of these studies, tax law changes have had clear and significant impacts on firm capital structure decisions. The effects of more permanent features of the tax code are considered next.

If taxes have an important influence on corporate capital structure decisions, then significant differences in national tax codes should be reflected in different capital structure patterns and in different market reactions to new financing decisions across countries. Consistent with this observation, Eckbo and Masulis found that announcements of standby rights offerings on average receive significantly negative stock price reactions in the United States while Marsh as well as Loderer and Zimmerman document positive stock price reactions to these announcements in Britain and Switzerland.[27]

Some preliminary evidence on international comparisons of firm capital structures and major differences in these sample countries' financial environments which could have capital structure implications is presented by Rutterford.[28] She examines differences in aggregate corporate leverage ratios across five major industrial economies, specifically: France, West Germany, Japan, Britain, and the United States, after adjusting for differential biases in leverage ratios caused by differences in accounting treatment across these countries. Rutterford then considers the basic differences in the tax structures and contractual arrangements that potentially could give rise to the observed differences in aggregate leverage ratios. She suggests that the higher leverage ratios found in Japan, and to a lesser extent in France and Germany, appear most consistent with the special contractual arrangements between corporate borrowers and institutional lenders in these countries, which lessen the conflict of interest between lenders and borrowers. To a great extent this conclusion reflects the fact that Rutterford finds it difficult to assess the net tax effects of corporate issuance of debt versus equity across these countries, especially once the effects of differences in nondebt tax shields are entertained.[29]

Fooladi and Roberts analyze the differences in the personal and corporate tax treatment of preferred stock and debt in the United States and Canada.[30] They conclude that preferred stock dividends are less heavily taxed for corporate and individual investors in Canada, which they argue will cause a higher optimum level of preferred stock in Canadian firms. Fooladi and Roberts then compare the percentage of the gross proceeds of security offerings represented by preferred stock in the United States and Canada annually. Over a recent ten-year period, preferred stock averaged 24.2 percent of gross proceeds in Canada and only 6.4 percent in the United States, which they argue supports their analysis.

In short, there is a wide variety of evidence supporting the significance of taxes in corporate financial decisions. Stock price reactions to announced changes in capital structure are found to be significantly related to changes in debt tax shield. Excess corporate tax shields are found to occur with substantial frequency and to persist over time. Changes in federal tax codes are found to cause rapid changes in corporate financial decisions. Firms in countries with different tax structures are observed to make different financial decisions and exhibit qualitatively different stock price reaction to the same financial decisions. These results support the relevance of tax-based models of optimal capital structure.

4

Costs of Bankruptcy and Financial Distress

Theoretical Aspects

Debt has a negative as well as a positive side. If debt rises significantly relative to firm assets, various added costs are incurred by the firm. In their mildest form, these costs are manifested in the unwillingness of customers and suppliers to do business with the firm except under less favorable terms. In more serious cases, debt holders can be asked to voluntarily forgo a portion of their claims so as to keep the firm solvent, thereby seriously hurting the firm's reputation with its lenders and often necessitating representation of debt holders on the board of directors. As leverage rises further, the firm can experience technical default or, in the extreme, economic insolvency, forcing it to file under a Chapter 10 or 11 of the Bankruptcy Act with sizable litigation and court costs.

Firms obviously would like to avoid the costs of financial distress, but economic downturns and declines in earnings cannot always be anticipated. While the probability of bankruptcy is a positive function of firm leverage, it is affected by other conditions as well. For example, some technologies and products are associated with greater earnings variability than others, and under certain conditions this translates into a greater probability of bankruptcy (see, for example, Castanias, Green and Talmor, and

Kale and Noe.[1]) Unfortunately, no direct documentation of the correlation between earnings variability and firm bankruptcy frequencies currently exists.

Miller argues that expected bankruptcy costs are relatively insignificant and thus should not affect a firm's financing decision.[2] In contrast, more recent theories of capital structure such as DeAngelo and Masulis posit that both the net tax benefits of debt and the costs of financial distress enter into the firm's financing decision.[3] The latter model yields an optimal leverage position for each firm, where the expected marginal tax advantage of debt is equated to the expected marginal costs of bankruptcy. One of the predictions of this model is that firms with higher expected bankruptcy costs should have lower leverage, everything else being the same. Holding the probability of insolvency constant, there are several reasons why some firms could have smaller expected bankruptcy costs; for instance, a firm could have lower costs of renegotiating debt contracts because of (1) a small number of debt holders, (2) a coincidence of investors holding the firm's debt and equity, or (3) an expedited reorganization process, as is the case for depository institutions.

Titman analyzes an issue closely related to bankruptcy: the impact of debt policy on a firm's liquidation decision.[4] He observes that, ex post, liquidation of a firm can benefit stockholders and bondholders by allowing the firm to break various implicit or explicit commitments with employees, customers, or suppliers. Titman observes that these affiliated parties can be materially hurt by a firm's liquidation. Since there can be a casual link between bankruptcy and the liquidation decision, these groups expect to be hurt if the firm falls into financial distress. Given their risks of losses under liquidation, stockholders can in times of financial distress extract concessions from the various parties with contractual ties to the firm so as to avoid bankruptcy. A good example is the concessions extracted from the suppliers, employees and dealers of International Harvester.[5] Titman argues that these risks cause financially weak firms to suffer significant losses in revenue prior to bankruptcy because of the adverse reactions of these suppliers, employees, and customers to increases in their risk of future losses.

Titman and Shapiro suggest that the costs of financial distress yield a clear economic rationale for firms that maximize value to appear risk averse in choosing their operating and financial decisions.[6] Titman and Shapiro review a number of manifestations of this activity. Titman argues that this risk-averse behavior should be greater for firms producing relatively unique goods. The losses to such a firm's suppliers, customers, and employees from liquidation are greater because of higher costs, both in abrogating customer and employee contracts to supply specialized services and in customers losing specialized servicing for their products. Broadly speaking, the above effects can be viewed as special cases of more general agency costs (discussed in Chapter 5) which are intensified by financial distress.

Evidence on the Costs of Bankruptcy and Financial Distress

Studies of bankruptcy costs have uncovered some important evidence on their relative significance. In a 1977 study of eleven railroad bankruptcies, Warner found the size of direct bankuptcy costs relative to firm value to be quite small (that is, averaging 1.4 percent five years prior and rising to 5.3 percent just prior to the bankruptcy filing).[7] These percentage costs appear to decrease with firm size. Given the small sample size, the regulated nature of the industry, and the special bankruptcy procedure followed by railroads, there is a serious question as to how generalizable this evidence can be.

However, in a 1984 study, Altman reports that the direct plus indirect bankruptcy costs tend to be substantially larger for industrial firms.[8] Altman defines the direct costs of bankruptcy as those explicitly paid by the debtors in the bankruptcy and reorganization process and the indirect costs of bankruptcy as those costs related to the loss of customers, suppliers, and employees, and the expenditure of managerial energies resulting from the firm's poor financial health. He estimates these indirect costs from the difference between current firm sales and the product of the firm's historical fraction of industry sales and current industry sales, all multiplied by the firm's historical profit margin. While this is most likely an overstatement of these costs, it is nevertheless a useful estimate.[9]

From a sample of recent bankruptcies by nineteen retail and other industrial firms, Altman found that the average direct costs of bankruptcy represent 6.0 percent of firm value both at the time of filing and five years prior. His estimates for the indirect bankruptcy costs plus direct costs as a fraction of firm value averaged 12.1 percent of firm value three years prior and 16.7 percent at the bankruptcy filing date. Even adjusting for the probability of bankruptcy, the expected time until it occurs, and the likelihood that the indirect costs of bankruptcy are somewhat overstated, this evidence indicates that expected costs of bankruptcy and of financial distress are too large to be ignored when firms make capital structure decisions.

Castanias argues that a useful alternative measure of a firm's bankruptcy probability is the frequency of insolvency in its industry.[10] With this measure, he goes on to test whether firms act as if they have optimal leverage ratios that involve trading off the net tax advantages of debt with the expected bankruptcy cost disadvantage. If they do, then firms with higher probabilities of bankruptcy should choose lower leverage ratios, everything else the same. Castanias examines the relationship between industry failure rates and leverage measures for a sample of smaller firms and finds that firms in industries with relatively high failure rates tend to have lower leverage. Litzenberger examines the valuation effects of two oil company restructurings that substantially increased firm leverage.[11] He presents evidence that these extreme leverage decisions lowered firm value. Further evidence documenting a negative relation between earnings variability and leverage is discussed in Chapter 9 of this book.

The evidence cited of substantive costs associated with bankruptcy as well as financial distress supports the relevance of these variables to a firm's financing decisions. The significance of these financial distress costs to a firm's capital structure decisions is supported further by evidence that firms with riskier earnings prospects have lower leverage. This evidence is inconsistent with Miller's leverage irrelevance theory, which assumes that these costs are insignificant.

5

Debt/Equity Agency Costs

Theoretical Review

The risk of bankruptcy and financial distress highlights the fact that conflicts of interest between stockholders and various fixed-payment claimants exist. These conflicts exist because the firm's fixed claims bear default risk while stockholders have limited liability residual claims and influence the managerial decision process. As a result, changes in firm asset and capital structures that change default risk can oppositely affect the values of these two classes of claimants. While these conflicts are greatest in periods of financial distress, they exist regardless of the firm's financial condition.

The implications of the stockholder-bondholder conflict of interest have been explored by a number of researchers, including Fama and Miller, Galai and Masulis, Jensen and Meckling, Myers, and Smith and Warner.[1] The consistent message in these papers is that these conflicts create incentives for stockholders to take actions that benefit themselves at the expense of bondholders and that do not necessarily maximize firm value.

Galai and Masulis analyze the conflict of interest between debt and equity owners, taking the perspective that the common stock of a levered firm is equivalent to a European call option.[2] They demonstrate that stockholders gain when the risk of firm assets is raised unexpectedly, even though the value of the firm's assets may fall. This result can occur because the risk increase causes a shift in wealth from bondholders to stockholders that more than offsets the effect of a fall in firm value on the stockholders. Thus, maximizing stockholders' wealth is not always equivalent to maximizing firm value, and if stockholders control the firm, the former objective is likely to be followed at the expense of the latter.[3] Galai and Masulis also demonstate how easily wealth transfers to stockholders can be effected through an increase in outstanding debt, a distribution of assets to stockholders (a spin-off), or a divestiture of low-risk assets.[4]

Jensen and Meckling argue that rational investors are aware of these conflicts and of the possible actions firms can take against bondholders.[5] Thus, when bonds are issued they are discounted immediately for the expected losses these anticipated actions would induce. This discounting means that, on average, stockholders do not gain from these actions, but firms consistently suffer by making suboptimal decisions for the purposes of ex post transfers of wealth to stockholders. Hence, incentives are created for firms to offer investors protective covenants, which limit the possible actions that would transfer wealth from debt holders to equity holders. However, the extent of these protective covenants is limited by the contracting technology, which determines the costs of originating, monitoring, and enforcing these covenants. For instance, protective covenants are often based on existing accounting numbers, which are easily monitored. These covenants create management incentives to make capital structure changes that produce artificial accounting gains for the purpose of weakening the covenant protection. In short, debt and equity conflicts of interest can be reduced but not eliminated by existing contracting technology.

Myers argues that a firm has two basic types of assets: tangible assets whose returns are unaffected by further investment, and growth opportunities whose returns are substantially enhanced by subsequent discretionary investment.[6] However, in certain circumstances, the gain from investment in growth opportunities can go primarily to bondholders (in states of bankruptcy), making these opportunities less attractive to firms seeking to maximize stockholders' wealth. More generally, the greater the proportion of growth assets, the easier it is to alter a firm's market value and risk to benefit stockholders at bondholders' expense.

Thus, firms with greater proportions of growth assets have greater conflicts of interest between stockholders and bondholders and therefore bear greater agency costs at the same level of leverage. Two predictions from this analysis are that firms with higher proportions of discretionary assets should on average have lower leverage and employ greater percentages of short-term debt (which is relatively immune to these wealth transfers due to its frequent renegotiation).

The agency costs arising from the inherent conflict of interest between stockholders and bondholders have implications for the existence of various features of debt contracts. Smith and Warner and, later, Green show that issuing convertible debt (or warrants) can lessen stockholders' incentive to support investment in projects that are unprofitable but increase firm risk.[7] Since convertible debt holders have the right to convert their debt claims into stock, they share in most positive wealth transfers to stockholders and also gain from any rise in the stock's total risk. Stockholders therefore have fewer opportunities to profitably expend corporate resources on actions that would enhance stock value at the expense of bondholders. Thus, the agency costs resulting from this conflict of interest often can be lowered with the use of this conversion feature.

Bodie and Taggart as well as Thatcher argue that call provisions in debt contracts can lower stockholder-bondholder agency costs.[8] Because certain low-risk but profitable projects primarily benefit bondholders, they will be rejected by the firm's stockholders. However, with early call provisions on the bonds, the gain to bondholders from investing in these projects is limited to the call premium. This feature allows the stockholders to capture a larger portion of the gain from undertaking profitable low-risk investment projects. Also, the value of the call provision to stockholders declines with a fall in firm value, making high-risk but unprofitable projects less attractive to stockholders as a way of effecting wealth transfers from bondholders. In short, inclusion of a call feature in a debt issue can increase firm value by reducing agency costs, even though the bonds' offering prices will be lowered by their inclusion.

Call provisions also involve negotiation and enforcement costs of their own, which limits their profitable application. In this regard, agency cost benefits are likely to be greatest in firms with high leverage and large proportions of intangible or growth assets. Accordingly, these contract features would most likely be found in a longer term, unsecured, and more junior debt issue since these are the issues with the greatest chance of large wealth transfers.

One specialized form of contract protection is represented by secured debt. Secured debt involves a transfer of title of pledged assets to the debt holders until the debt is fully redeemed. There are many variations on this basic idea, including equipment trusts, mortgages, pension funds, repurchase agreements, and leases. The costs and benefits of issuing secured debt are explored by Stulz and Johnson.[9] They formally prove that there are contracting cost savings from using secured debt in overcoming the underinvestment problem. An underinvestment problem can occur when the existing unsecured debt holders are the major beneficiary of new investment, thereby discouraging stockholders from supporting the undertaking. Giving new secured debt holders first claim to these new investments limits the gains realized by the outstanding unsecured debt and increases the gains to stockholders by increasing the market price of the new debt being issued.

Smith and Warner consider secured debt as a means of lowering loan interest rates by precluding the substitution of riskier assets for some of the firm's existing assets, hence decreasing administrative and enforcement costs of debt contracts.[10] Myers and Majluf argue that secured debt can help overcome the agency costs associated with investor uncertainty about firm assets in place by giving investors collateral in the firm's more easily valued tangible assets.[11] One implication of this analysis is that secured debt is more beneficial as the riskiness of the existing debt rises and as uncertainty about the assets in place increases.

Lease contracts can be viewed as a strong form of secured debt where the lender receives legal claim to the secured assets at the time of the loan. Smith and Wakeman, in studying the conflicts of interest between lessor and lessee, develop some interesting conclusions as to what assets are better suited to be leased.[12] They argue that assets best suited for leasing arrangements (1) have market values that are relatively insensitive to lessee use and maintenance decisions (which are difficult to monitor), so that the asset's market value over the contract period can be easily assessed, and (2) are not specialized to the firm so that its repossession value is relatively high. These asset characteristics also are desirable ones for the collateral of other secured debt contracts.

Pension liabilities can be interpreted as a form of secured debt in the sense that these liabilities have first claim to the assets of the firm's pension fund. They differ in that (1) the level of vested liabilities generally exceeds the value of pension fund assets, (2) covenants (primarily determined by the Employee Retirement Income Security Act of 1974 (ERISA)) protecting liability holders are very limited, and (3) liability holders receive partial insurance from the Pension Benefit Guaranty Corporation (PBGC), based on a risk-insensitive premium structure. Stockholders have conflicting incentives in that pension contributions are tax-deductible, and pension fund earnings are tax-exempt, which encourages overfunding, while the PBGC's risk-insensitive premium structure and pension holders' weak protective covenants encourage underfunding and investment in riskier financial claims. There is also some risk of expropriation of overfunded plans by pensioner suits and by PBGC levying higher premiums on strong funds. For a more formal analysis of optimal corporate pension funding policy, see Harrison and Sharpe as well as Bicksler and Chen.[13]

In general, the partitioning of debt into separate classes with differing rights creates the potential for conflict of interest among these various classes of debt holders. These conflicts can be exacerbated at times of financial distress because of the bankruptcy court's penchant for overriding the absolute priority rule that requires senior claimants to be paid off in full before more junior claimants can be paid. Some of the implications of this issue have been explored by Warner and by Masulis.[14]

The importance of time priority as well as seniority to a debt issue's value and the conflicts of interest they create are highlighted in Bulow and Shoven's study of a firm in financial distress with three classes of securities outstanding: common stock, short-term debt, and long-term debt.[15] They show that when a firm has negative net worth stockholders will not buy additional stock to enable the firm to avoid bankruptcy, but short-term debt holders may extend additional credit in exchange for partial payment of their existing claims so that the firm can avoid default. This action can benefit the short-term debt (as well as the stock), since it enables the firm to avoid the costs of bankruptcy and preserves the time priority of short-term debt (it is paid off sooner provided that no default occurs). If bankruptcy were declared, then the long-term debt's claim would be accelerated and if this claim had senior or equal standing, its priority could lessen the payoff to short-term debt holders.[16]

Thus, there are reasons for at least some classes of debt to support a renegotiation of their claims when the firm is in financial distress. This conflict of interest among debt holders may also explain the prominence of sinking fund requirements in long-term corporate debt issues. The sinking fund requirement lowers the probability of default at the long-term debt's distant maturity date, after most of the short-term debt has been redeemed, and increases the bankruptcy probability somewhat at earlier sinking fund dates. This feature effectively spreads the longer term debt's maturity over time, thereby eliminating much of the time priority advantage of the shorter term debt issue.

Evidence on the Effects of Conflicts of Interest among Firm Claimants

Evidence on the impacts of a debt/equity conflict of interest comes in many forms. The clearest evidence is the pervasiveness of comprehensive protective covenants in debt contracts, as documented by Smith and Warner.[17] They analyze standard indenture features of public issues of corporate debt in terms of the potential actions stockholders can take to transfer wealth away from bondholders. Smith and Warner classify these actions into four major categories: (1) increases in dividend payouts and other asset distributions to stockholders; (2) claim dilution, that is, increases in debt of equal or senior standing; (3) asset substitution, or the replacement of less risky collateral with riskier assets; and (4) underinvestment, or the rejection of positive net present value projects when the benefits accrue to bondholders, and overinvestment, or the acceptance of negative net present value projects when gains to stockholders ensue.

Smith and Warner analyze how standard covenants protect against each of the four types of actions. Taking a random sample of eighty-seven indentures filed with the SEC in 1974–1975, Smith and Warner found that 91 percent contained restrictions against the issuance of additional debt, 36 percent contained restrictions on the disposition of assets, and only 23 percent contained restrictions on dividends per se. They observed that issues of lower priority debt and debt issues of firms in weaker financial condition have stricter and more extensive protective covenants.[18]

Suprisingly, some of the largest and financially strong firms have extremely weak protective covenants as documented in a recent paper by McDaniel, who surveys the debt covenants of the one hundred largest U.S. industrial corporations.[19] He reports that of the ninety-two companies in this sample with one or more senior or subordinated issues, only 28 percent had restrictions on unsecured long-term debt issuance, only 35 percent had restrictions on dividends, and none had restrictions on the disposition of assets. This evidence suggests that while the widespread existence of protective covenants should lessen the manifestations of this debt/equity conflict of interest, the protection afforded by these covenants is far from complete, which no doubt reflects the costs of negotiating and implementing these covenants.

Three corporate finance studies which report evidence that debtholders have borne significant losses as a result of weak protective covenants are by Kim, McConnell, and Greenwood, by Masulis, and by Litzenberger.[20] They document evidence concerning several relatively infrequent firm actions that appear to benefit stockholders at the expense of debt holders.[21]

The study by Kim, McConnell, and Greenwood analyzes common stock and debt price reactions to the formation of captive financing company subsidiaries. The formation of these financing companies has the effect of raising firm leverage, and their announcements are associated with positive stock price changes and negative bond price changes. While the authors offer no direct evidence, over the period studied the formation of captive subsidiaries was a relatively new means of increasing leverage which covenants of existing debt issues were unlikely to protect against.

In a separate study, Masulis found that when existing debt covenants fail to prohibit the issuance of debt of equal or senior standing (unusually weak protective covenants are almost entirely associated with debt issued in earlier mergers or recapitalizations), and the firm announces an exchange offer of senior debt for existing equity, on average there are positive stock price changes and negative debt price changes. Pinegar and Lease reexamined the earlier evidence by Masulis on the effects of preferred-for-common exchange offers and report further evidence of wealth redistributions between the holders of preferred and common stock.[22]

Litzenberger analyzes two case studies of major capital restructurings by oil companies. He finds in both cases that the announcements of large increases in debt associated with these actions appeared to cause decreases in the market values of company debt issues.[23] Lehn and Poulsen, in a study of leveraged buyouts, report that holders of nonconvertible bonds do not share in the price gains experienced by the holders of common stock and that many bond issues suffer rating reduction.[24] Two studies of issuer tender offers for common stock by Masulis and Dann also have uncovered some weak evidence that, on average, holders of nonconvertible debt experience small negative returns, while holders of common stock experience large positive returns at the time of these announcements.[25] One can conclude from this body of evidence that while the manifestations of the debt/equity conflict of interest may be relatively infrequent, the actual conflict of interest is pervasive.[26]

Mayers and Smith examine the causes and effects of stock life insurance companies changing to a mutual form of organization.[27] They argue that mutualization reduces the conflicts of interest between policyholders and mutual owners, since mutual owners receive more limited gains from corporate risk-taking (which can hurt policyholders) than is the case in stock companies. Insurance companies that initially had proportionately high management stock ownership are subsequently reported to realize larger percentage growth in premium income. They interpret this as evidence that mutualization leads to a reduction in the agency costs of policyholder-owner conflicts of interest, which increases demand for policies. They argue that these gains exceed any efficiency losses from lessening the market discipline exerted on managers. They also find that existing stockholders in all but one case received sizable premiums from tendering their shares to the firm. Based on this and other evidence. Mayers and Smith conclude that all major parties in a stock insurance company (stockholders, policyholders, and managers) gain from the mutualization. There is also evidence of wealth gains by managers at the expense of outside stockholders.

To assess the validity of the agency-theory predictions concerning debt and preferred stock conversion rights, evidence is needed concerning the characteristics of firms issuing convertible bonds and convertible preferred stocks and the particular security classes that have these conversion features (casual evidence suggests that it is generally unsecured junior debt). For example, debt of regulated firms might seem less likely to include conversion features because monitoring by regulators helps protect the debt holders from having their position undercut and limits the gains the stockholders could obtain. However, no careful study of these various questions currently is available.

Likewise, there is also a need for evidence on the frequency and extent of secured debt across firms, including equipment trusts and mortgages. Firms relying heavily on lease contracts, which are also very close to secured debt (although the tax implications are different and the residual claim is owned by the lender) deserve further study.[28] The relationships between short-term debt and other firm characteristics such as the proportion of tangible assets and the extent of growth opportunities also would be of interest.

A body of evidence has been accumulated on the implications of agency costs for other features of debt contracts. Thatcher observes that agency theory predicts that firms with either greater discretion over investment decisions, or outstanding debt that is more sensitive to changes in firm value, are more likely to suffer from the asset substitution and the underinvestment problems, which a debt call provision would partially relieve.[29] She reports that in comparing the characteristics of firms and their debt issues by whether they include or exclude early call provisions, significant differences are observed. Debt issues with early call provisions were found to have significantly longer years to maturity and more often to be unsecured. The firms calling one or more of their debt issues early were observed to have higher leverage, lower profitability, and higher average maturity for outstanding debt. However, no significant difference in the growth rate of assets was observed. With the exception of the last result, this evidence supports the predictions of the agency cost arguments Thatcher presents.

One intriguing piece of evidence relating to secured debt is reported in a study of debt offerings by Eckbo.[30] He separately analyzes the stock price reaction to announcements of mortgage bond offerings, a form of secured debt, from announcements of other nonconvertible debt offerings. Eckbo finds that the average stock returns associated with mortgage bond offering announcements were three times more negative than the returns associated with unsecured nonconvertible bond offering announcements. This evidence seems inconsistent with arguments promoting the benefits of secured debt. However, this result is consistent with secured debt announcements releasing negative information about the financial condition of these firms that outweighs the direct benefit from using this form of debt.

The conflicts of interest between stockholders and pension holders are illustrated most clearly by considering how ERISA altered funding of pension liabilities and the investment of fund assets in a firm's own securities (an action that pierces the secured nature of the pension claim). Prior to ERISA, many corporations had plans that were both underfunded and heavily invested in the firms' own stock, which effectively overstates the funding level by the value of this stock investment.[31] With the passage of ERISA many manifestations of this conflict of interest are now prohibited. However, investment of up to 10 percent of pension fund assets in the firm's own stock remains legal, and other manifestations of these conflicts are still observed, such as the discretion in determining the riskiness of the pension fund portfolio, in choosing the actuarial method used to determine the necessary level of funding, and the loaning of funds to the corporation at below-market rates (for evidence of this activity see Feldstein and Morck and Bodie et al.[32]). Recent evidence on plan takeovers by PBGC, where limited insurance coverage is guaranteed, indicates that stockholders can still gain at the expense of pension liability holders and the PBGC.[33]

Feldstein and Seligman, Daley, and Landsman report indirect evidence that off-balance-sheet unfunded vested pension liabilities are reflected in lower stock prices, but such that for each additional dollar of pension liability there is less than one dollar reduction of equity.[34] This evidence is consistent with pension liabilities being risky or market anticipation of a partial payment of the liability by an outside third party, namely PBGC.

In a study of the tax and agency relationships associated with pensions, Bodie et al. report that the extent of funding for vested pension liabilities is positively related to a firm's profitability and its tax-paying status, but they find no significant relation with firm risk.[35] This evidence appears to support the previous tax arguments but not the PBGC insurance subsidy argument. However, both Black and Tepper argue that tax-exempt pension funds should invest solely in fully taxable but low-risk assets such as corporate and government bonds if a tax discount exists in these security prices and the PBGC subsidy on risk-taking is insignificant.[36] Yet, Tepper finds that often more than half of pension fund assets have been in riskier but more lightly taxed stock investments. This observation is consistent with the tax benefits of low-risk bond investment being dominated by the risk subsidy benefit of PBGC. Confirmation of this conjecture is lacking. Also needed is clear evidence of the extent to which unfunded pension liabilities influence a firm's leverage decision.

Studies of the effects of conflicts of interest among various debt classes are currently unavailable. Nevertheless, the number of articles in the business press describing the major disagreements among classes of debt holders of firms in reorganization is sizable and indicates that serious delays in leaving bankruptcy status can result. These delays imply additional court costs and legal fees and also can result in additional indirect costs of the bankruptcy proceedings.

Overall, the evidence documents a broad range of situations where conflicts of interest among equity holders and debt holders (including lessors and pensioners) manifest themselves and where their impacts on firm capital structures are significant. Protective covenants are standard features of debt contracts, but even with their existence a number of wealth redistributions adversely affecting debt holders have been recorded. There is also evidence that the existence of various debt contract features such as convertibility, call features, sinking funds, and securitization are, in part, an effort to lower the agency costs associated with this debt/equity conflict of interest.

6

Stockholder-Manager Conflicts of Interest

Review of the Theories

The conflict of interest between a principal and an agent with operating responsibility and better information on the quality and extent of the firm's investment opportunities or the economic value of its stock is a well-known problem in economics. It has spawned a large literature considering the best incentive contract for agents to align their interests with those of the principals, taking into account the efficiency loss associated with a particular contract choice. One of the important issues explored by this literature is the set of ex post observable variables that could be used in an incentive contract to modify a manager's fixed wage compensation. A parallel finance literature associated with Jensen and Meckling also has developed, which emphasizes the contracting cost associated with the inherent conflict of interest between outside stockholders and a firm's manager who has superior information about his efforts or perquisite consumption and has a simple compensation contract defined as a percentage holding of stock.[1]

The conflict between stockholders and managers takes four principal forms:

1. Managers prefer greater perquisite levels and lower effort levels, provided that they do not have to pay for the full cost through lower wages or a lower market value for their personal stock holdings.
2. Managers prefer less risky investments and lower leverage to lessen the probability of bankruptcy, an event that would adversely affect their current and future compensation and subject their relatively undiversified portfolios to large losses in stock value.
3. Managers prefer investments with shorter horizons at the expense of more profitable long-term projects.
4. Managers prefer to minimize the likelihood of employment termination, which increases with changes in corporate control.[2]

Manager-stockholder conflicts of interest can be mitigated by substantially altering management compensation contracts and through the discipline imposed by competition in product markets and in the markets for corporate control and managerial labor. A substantial literature has developed which considers the optimal structure of managerial compensation contracts needed to mitigate the effects of these conflicts. In addition, the tax code also has been recognized as influencing the structure of these incentive contracts. Given the extent of managerial decision-making powers, these managerial compensation contracts represent an important component of a firm's capital structure.

The extent to which the market for corporate control disciplines management is closely related to the distribution of voting rights across shareholders and the proportion of outstanding shares held by the management group. Demsetz and Lehn argue that increasing the concentration of stockholders improves the effectiveness and lowers the cost of stockholders' monitoring of management decisions.[3] They also argue that as stability of profits rises and as government regulation intensifies, stockholder-borne costs of obtaining the same level of monitoring of management actions falls, which reduces manager-stockholder agency costs.[4] Thus, another significant element of a firm's capital structure decisions is the distribution of voting rights across investors.

Grossman and Hart develop a principal-agent model where leverage can be used as a bonding mechanism to reduce management discretion and thus lessen a manager's potential opportunistic behavior.[5] Since leverage increases the probability of bankruptcy, which is costly to managers, leverage can be used as an effective certification device for manager quality. Thus, increasing leverage is predicted in the Grossman-Hart model to increase firm value and presumably its stock value as well.

Extending the earlier agency theory literature, Jensen argues that managers have strong incentives to increase firm size because their salaries and prestige are positively related to size.[6] This incentive creates a conflict of interest between the expansionary-minded manager and stockholders seeking to maximize the value of their shares. To obtain external funds for expansion, the manager must pass the scrutiny of the external capital market, where weak investment plans can meet with public criticism, and in extreme cases, portend offering failure. However, if a sufficient amount of unencumbered internal funds is on hand, the manager can more easily undertake less profitable projects with a minimum of external monitoring. It follows that the values of cash-rich firms that are undertaking unprofitable expansion will be heavily discounted, and as a consequence they will make tempting takeover targets.

Jensen argues that if stockholders could effectively bond management not to undertake unprofitable expansionary actions, a firm's value would be enhanced and its attractiveness as a takeover target would be diminished. For example, one source of discretionary funds is the surplus assets in overfunded pension plans, whose elimination would improve the bonding of management. Jensen suggests several long-term methods of potentially bonding a manager. The expected dividend payout could be increased, or the firm's debt load could be raised, thereby lowering "free cash flow" where the latter action is more binding since the firm cannot decrease its debt payments without risking a bankruptcy proceeding. A third alternative for lowering the discretionary funds available to management is a leveraged buyout (LBO), which in many ways is an extreme form of the two previous alternatives. In essence, Jensen views the firm's dividend policy and capital structure as acting as effective internal restraints on management's unprofitable expansionary tendencies. Interestingly, Jensen assumes away the use of managerial incentive contracts as a useful vehicle for aligning manager interests with shareholders in favor of externally visible bonding mechanisms. It is also in stark contrast to Fama's argument that the managerial labor market will exert strong discipline on managers' behavior.[7]

Kensinger and Martin argue that corporate reorganization into royalty trusts or limited partnership is an alternative and potentially more effective way of minimizing the manager-stockholder agency costs.[8] They observe that unlike corporate management, the managing partner in a limited partnership is only charged with the efficient operation of *existing* enterprises, and as such has limited discretion in dividend/reinvestment matters. Moreover, in a limited partnership, revenues and expenses are credited directly to the partners' individual accounts according to a fixed contractual formula. In these organizations, the decision to reinvest profits resides with each individual investor and generally is not a decision under the control of management as it is in a corporation. So the manager-stockholder agency costs are lowered by taking away much of management's decision-making power. In addition to this potential agency benefit, royalty trusts and limited partnerships have had significant tax benefits over ordinary corporations. While the approaches advocated by Jensen and by Kensinger and Martin may seem a bit extreme, less dramatic contractual arrangements to alter management incentives also are available and are in widespread use as discussed below.

Smith and Watts summarize typical provisions of managerial compensation contracts and analyze how they help control the conflicts of interest of managers and stockholders.[9] These contracts are separated into three major components:

1. Compensation that does not depend on corporate performance

2. Compensation that depends on market-based measures of corporate performance
3. Compensation that depends on accounting-based measures of corporate performance

All of these major components of managerial incentive contracts have the effect of increasing the alignment of manager incentives with those of stockholders.

Fixed compensation, such as wages and pensions set at the start of the period, do nothing to alleviate this conflict of interest with stockholders. However, fixed compensation does allow the level of firm-specific risk borne by management to have some limit, by having the firm guarantee some minimum level of compensation independent of firm fortunes.

Market-based compensation, such as stock and "phantom stock" (where the manager is credited with shares and at the end of a specified period is paid their market value in cash), is well suited for controlling the perquisite consumption and the horizon problems, since perquisite consumption and less profitable short-term investments adversely affect stock price. Stock options and stock appreciation rights help control the managerial risk-aversion problem since their values are positively related to firm risk and leverage.[10]

Accounting-based compensation is especially useful for rewarding division-level managers on the basis of individual division performance. It is superior to stock-based compensation, because stock price can be insensitive to the decisions of the division managers, but the accounting profits of the division will be much more closely related to these managers' performance. An interesting variant on this theme is a performance share contract. In these contracts lower level management are rewarded with bonuses based on accounting objectives, but these bonuses are paid in shares of the firm's stock.

The potential conflicts of interest between stockholders and managers have some other important implications as well. Dann and DeAngelo note that various asset structure and capital structure changes can be motivated by management efforts to deter hostile takeover bids even at the expense of firm value, as is epitomized by the merger and acquisition term, "scorched earth policy."[11] Certain "going-private" actions and conversions to mutual organization also can be motivated by potential takeover threats. Given this motivation for some capital structure changes, announcements of these decisions at times act as signals to the market of an opportunity to share in a takeover or buyout premiums, thereby causing positive stock price reactions for reasons independent of the direct effects of the capital structure change.

Major capital structure changes also can be motivated by the objective of substantially changing management compensation or risk-bearing in the firm. For example, leveraged buyouts can increase management's equity investment and risk-bearing, while converting from mutual to stock charter can enable managers to obtain stock and stock option positions in a firm. In reviewing the following evidence, these other potential implications of capital structure change need to be kept in mind.

Empirical Evidence on the Stockholder-Manager Conflict of Interest

Conflicts of interest between management and stockholders are at their greatest at times of corporate control contests. In such situations stockholders often stand to gain substantial premiums from supporting a takeover, while management faces the prospect of uncertain tenure at best. Evidence consistent with managers' making capital structure changes to deter potential takeovers contrary to current shareholder interests is reported by Bradley and Wakeman, Dann and DeAngelo, and Malatesta and Walkling.[12] In all of these studies, the announcement of block (targeted) repurchases of stock or of other capital structure or charter changes that discourage hostile bidders is on average greeted by negative price adjustments in the target firms' common stocks. The negative market reaction is most pronounced when stockholder approval of these defensive actions is not required. This evidence seems to indicate that management incentive contracts are not always effective in eliminating the manager-stockholder conflict of interest.

There is currently little direct evidence on the effects of management bonding through the use of debt or dividend policies.

Jensen observes that the positive market reactions to announcement of cash dividend changes reported by Charest and by Aharony and Swary are consistent with the theory.[13] Evidence of positive market reactions to issuer tender offers, stock repurchase programs, leveraged buyouts, and other leverage-increasing decisions and the nonpositive market reactions to external financing decisions is also indirect support for the bonding argument. Somewhat less encouraging, Asquith and Mullins report that stock price reactions to equity offerings are insignificantly related to changes in a measure of free cash flow (change in net debt).[14]

Demsetz and Lehn study the importance of stockholder concentration in ameliorating the effects of the manager-stockholder conflict of interest.[15] Based on a large sample of U.S. corporations, they report that concentration of stock ownership is negatively related to the stability in firm profits, the extent of government regulation, and firm size. This evidence is consistent with Demsetz and Lehn's analysis, which views the concentration of stockholders as a means of increasing the effectiveness of stockholders' monitoring of management and these other firm characteristics as decreasing the optimal level of shareholders' monitoring. One other supportive piece of evidence is by Wruck, who analyzes private placements of common stock.[16] She reports that these sales have the effect of increasing the concentration of outside stockholders and finds positive stock returns on their announcement. Further, she finds that the larger the block of shares sold in percentage terms, the greater the positive effect of the announcement.

Evidence on the extent to which management compensation plans act to align managers' interests with those of stockholders is developed by Murphy.[17] He studied the relationship between corporate performance and managerial compensation and found a strong positive relationship using either stockholders' returns or growth in firm sales as the measure of corporate performance.[18] This conclusion is not surprising given that the market-based component of managerial compensation is properly included in the analysis. However, the level of correlation reported by Murphy is surprisingly low. He reports that for a 10 percent change in equity value, there is only about a 2 percent change in managerial compensation. This evidence suggests that the compensation contracts do not come close to eliminating the stockholder-manager conflict of interest, although surely they lessen them.

The effectiveness of managerial compensation contracts in mitigating conflicts of interest with shareholders can be inferred from a number of sources. One type of evidence comes from studying changes in compensation plans in particular industries. Larcker examined changes in the level of employee and perquisite expenditures after the adoption of bonus contracts for a sample of major commercial banks.[19] He reports that the banks adopting these plans show some decrease in perquisite expenditures relative to their revenues. In two broader studies of U.S. firms, by Larcker and by Bhagat, Brickley, and Lease, the average stock market reaction to the adoption of market-based compensation plans was found to be statistically significant and positive for these firms' stocks.[20] Larcker also reports that, after the initial adoption of long-term performance plans, substantial increases in capital investment by these firms were observed relative to similar firms without these plans.

Wolfson examined the effects of bonus contracts on the behavior of executives in oil and gas partnerships.[21] In a typical bonus contract arrangement, an agency problem arises because the managing partner bears all the costs of well completion but must share the revenue with the limited partners. As a consequence, the managing partner actually can bear losses when the well is marginally profitable. One way to limit this conflict of interest is to limit exploration to highly risky well locations where discovery is unlikely but very profitable when it occurs. Wolfson reports that partnerships operating under this bonus contract arrangement engaged in significantly riskier drilling activities, as he would predict.

An alternative way of assessing the impact of long-term compensation plans is to consider the stock market reaction to their announcements. Several recent studies have analyzed firm actions that have the effect of substantially altering management stock ownership. DeAngelo, DeAngelo, and Rice explored the valuation effects of announcements of firms "going private" on the firms' common stock prices[22] In these actions, firm leverage is substantially increased, in turn raising stock risk while management's equity investment in the firm is significantly expanded. DeAngelo et al. interpret the large and significant gains to managers and outside stockholders at the time of these actions as supportive of the firms realizing efficiency gains from having managers take large equity positions in these highly levered firms.[23]

An alternative explanation for the result obtained by DeAngelo et al. is that the net tax benefits of debt combined with a smaller stockholder-bondholder agency cost, which results from having a small group of investors hold "strips" of claims to most or all of the firm's various debt and equity issues, yields a higher optimum leverage. This form of ownership structure is attractive because it minimzes the potential conflicts of interest among security holders and makes contract renegotiation relatively inexpensive, as is exemplified by Congoleum's well-known 1979 leverage buyout (see the Harvard Business School case study).[24] Downes and Heinkel studied the effects of another major capital structure decision, namely firms "going public."[25] They found that stock offering prices were positively related to the percentage of share ownership retained by firm management. To the extent that a larger ownership position mitigates the stockholder-manager agency problem, this observed higher offering price would be expected.

Masulis recently studied the effects of mutual savings and loan association (mutual S&L) conversions to stock charter.[26] This conversion process involves a regulatory required equity offering, which is similar to a firm going public. As a consequence, conversion to stock charter lowers an S&L's leverage ratio, which benefits the S&L's deposit insuror by lowering the S&L's risk of insolvency. Other S&L claimants benefit if the leverage decrease moves the S&L to a more optimal leverage position, which was unattainable as a mutually chartered S&L where equity offerings are infeasible. Conversion also enables management compensation to have stock and stock option components, which helps mitigate the inherent conflict of interest between managers and outside stockholders. This is, in part, due to the managers and board of directors being able to exchange limited ownership claims in the mutual association for stock options and rights to purchase common stock. In addition to the Federal Saving and Loan Insurance Corporation gaining from conversion, the depositors and managers subscribing to the stock offering on average realized a significant wealth gain from the conversion. In sum, this study finds that the conversion process, which increases market-based managerial compensation, is associated with increases in the market values of all the S&L's major liabilities and therefore in market value of the S&L itself.

Management's ownership of stock is predicted to positively affect firm value. Demsetz offers some interesting statistics concerning management and board of director stock ownership for a sample of large firms in the Fortune 500.[27] His evidence indicates that management or board ownership varies substantially across firms from 2.1 percent to 20.4 percent, with larger management ownership in smaller firms.

One way to assess the importance of management ownership on firm valuation is to analyze stock price reactions at the time of announced changes in ownership. A large body of event study evidence is detailed in Table 6-1 relating to this question. These studies consistently report average stock price reactions of the same sign as the announced changes in managment's proportional ownership of outstanding stock. For instance, firm actions that increase shares outstanding imply a decrease in management's fractional share ownership and are associated with stock price declines, while share repurchases generally imply an increase in management's percentage share ownership and are associated with stock price gains.

The previous body of evidence supports the prediction that increases in management share ownership generally increase firm value by lowering manager-stockholder conflicts of interest. To be more precise, this agency cost gain must more than offset any increase in compensation required by managers for bearing a greater level of firm-specific risk from its ownership of firm stock. In a recent study of management stockholding and corporate performance, Morck, Shleifer, and Vishny report that this performance is highest for firms with management stock holdings of between 5 and 20 percent of outstanding stock and drops off for larger or smaller levels.[28] Their primary measure of performance is the ratio of firm market value to replacement cost of its physical assets. This evidence indicates that at relatively high levels of management stock ownership, the agency cost gains previously discussed are offset by some additional costs. Possible explanations for this finding, when management stock ownership levels are high, are that the market for corporate control is ineffective in disciplining managers or that manager-owners are obtaining a tax-sheltered nonpecuniary return on their investments, which are treated as corporate expenses.

There is a further set of evidence that supports the agency interpretation of stock price effects detailed in Table 6–1. This evidence is based on cross-sectional regression estimates of the relationship between a management's fractional share ownership and firm value. Downes and Heinkel as well as Ritter study the relation between management's fractional share holdings and the market value of the firm's common stock subsequent to their initial public offerings for a large sample of cases.[29] Both studies report a statistically significant positive relationship after controlling for firms' current earnings and investment.

Vermaelen studies the relationships among stock returns on the announcement of issuer tender offers and several explanatory variables believed to represent signals of firm value.[30] These explanatory variables are management's initial fractional share holdings, the tender offer premium, and the target fraction of shares sought in the offer. Vermaelen reports that stock announcement returns have significant positive relationships to both management's initial fractional share holdings and the fraction of shares sought (which generally increases management's fractional ownership, since they are typically excluded from the offer). The evidence in all of these studies appears supportive of higher management fractional ownership decreasing the agency costs inherent in the manager-stockholder conflict of interest.

One last piece of evidence on the effects of management shareholding comes from a study of firm leverage ratios undertaken by Friend and Hasbrouck.[31] Regressing firm leverage ratios against tangible assets, profitability, risk of bankruptcy, firm size, and the market value of equity held by the dominant insider,

Table 6–1. Average Stock Price Reactions to Changes in Management's Fractional Ownership of Shares

Study	Type of Announcement	Sample Size	Two-Day Mean Ann. Ret. (%)
	Decreases in Management Share Ownership		
Masulis[a]	Exchange offers of common stock for debt	20	-9.9*,†
Finnerty[b]	Private swaps of common stock for debt	113	-1.1*
Peavy and Scott[c]	Private swaps of common stock for debt	93	-.6*
Rogers and Owers[d]	Private swaps of common stock for debt	74	-1.1*
Asquith and Mullins[e]	Seasoned primary common stock offerings	128	-3.0*
Mikkelson and Partch[f]	Seasoned primary common stock offerings	388	-3.3+
Masulis and Korwar[g]	Seasoned primary common stock offerings	80	-3.6*
Masulis and Korwar[g]	Combination primary-secondary offerings involving management sales	56	-4.6*
Mikkelson and Partch[f]	Secondary offerings of stock involving management sales	53	-3.4*
	Increases in Management Share Ownership		
DeAngelo, DeAngelo, and Rice[h]	Going-private transactions	72	28.3*
Masulis[i]	Conversions of mutual S&Ls to stock charter	78	7.6
Masulis[a]	Exchange offers of debt for common stock	52	14.0*,†
Masulis[j]	Common stock repurchase by tender offer	199	16.4*
Dann[k]	Common stock repurchase by tender offer	142	15.4*
Vermaelen[l]	Common stock repurchase by tender offer	131	14.1*

For footnotes see adjacent page.

Table 6–1. Average Stock Price Reactions to Changes in Management's Fractional Ownership of Shares (Continued)

a. Ronald W. Masulis, "Stock Repurchase by Tender Offer: An Analysis of the Causes of Common Stock Price Changes," *Journal of Finance* 35 (1980): 305–19.

b. John D. Finnerty, "Stock-for-Debt Swaps and Shareholder Returns," *Financial Management* 14 (1985): 5–17.

c. John W. Peavy and Jonathon A. Scott, "The Effect of Stock-for-Debt Swaps on Security Returns," *Financial Review* 20 (1985): 303–27.

d. Ronald C. Rogers and James E. Owers, "Equity for Debt Exchanges and Stockholder Wealth," *Financial Management* 14 (1985): 18–26.

e. Paul Asquith and David W. Mullins, "Equity Issues and Stock Price Dilution," *Journal of Financial Economics* 15 (1986): 61–89.

f. Wayne Mikkelson and Megan Partch, "Stock Price Effects and Costs of Secondary Distributions," *Journal of Financial Economics* 14 (1985): 165–94.

g. Ronald W. Masulis and Ashok W. Korwar, "Seasoned Equity Offerings: An Empirical Investigation," *Journal of Financial Economics* 15 (1986): 91–118.

h. Harry DeAngelo, Linda DeAngelo, and Edward M. Rice, "Going Private: Minority Freezeouts and Shareholder Wealth," *Journal of Law and Economics* 27 (1984): 367–401.

i. Ronald W. Masulis, "Changes in Ownership Structure: Conversions of Mutual Savings and Loans to Stock Charter," *Journal of Financial Economics* 18 (1987): 29–59.

j. Ronald W. Masulis, "The Effect of Capital Structure Change on Security Prices: A Study of Exchange Offers," *Journal of Financial Economics* 8 (1980): 139–77.

k. Larry Dann, "Common Stock Repurchases: An Analysis of Returns to Bondholders and Stockholders," *Journal of Financial Economics* 9 (1981): 113–38.

l. Theo Vermaelen, "Common Stock Repurchases and Market Signalling," *Journal of Financial Economics* 9 (1981): 139–83.

*Statistically significant at the 5 percent level.

†Stock returns include the initial announcement period and in 40 percent of the sample a second return representing a clarifying announcement.

they find that all these variables have significant parameter estimates. The distinguishing feature of this study is its inclusion of share holdings of the dominant insider and the fact that this variable has a significantly negative parameter estimate. Friend and Hasbrouck interpret this result as indicative of a manager-stockholder agency problem, resulting from the inability of the dominant insiders to diversify adequately the risk of their stock holdings. As a result, risk aversion can cause the dominant stockholder to choose a leverage ratio lower than the value-maximizing level preferred by outside investors who can diversify firm-specific risk easily. Furthermore, this tendency generally increases with the size of the insider's stock holdings.

In summary, evidence supports the existence of a stockholder-manager conflict of interest, which is especially severe at times of corporate control contests. Indirect evidence that leverage increases and dividend payouts help bond managers to act in shareholders' interests is observed. Corporate reorganizations that substantially increase management share holdings, and therefore their firm-specific risk bearing, appear to increase firm values. Managerial incentive contracts are found to help align (although imperfectly) management's interests with those of stockholders. Finally, larger proportions of stock ownership by management appear to reduce the agency costs of this conflict of interest.

7

Information Implicit in Capital Structure Adjustment Decisions

Theoretical Overview

Since capital structure changes are managerial responses to changes in a firm's current and expected economic condition, its outside environment, or both, these choices can impart information to the market about management's expectations for the firm. This information is in addition to any direct effects that capital structure decisions may have. This view was first formalized by Ross, who went on to argue that managers have incentives to employ capital structure changes (specifically leverage changes) as signals to the market of like changes in firm earnings prospects.[1] These are credible signals, because if future increases in cash flows do not materialize after leverage is increased, there is a bankruptcy cost penalty to be borne by the firm and its managers.[2]

Leland and Pyle proposed a signaling model that predicts that changes in management's stock holdings reflect like changes in firm value.[3] The explanation is that investors assume correctly that management is better informed about expected cash flows and that, from the standpoint of diversification, it is costly for risk-averse managers to hold a significant fraction of firm stock. Thus, managers have incentives to hold large stock positions only if they expect future cash flows to be high relative to the firm's current market value. Therefore, rational investors will consider managers' equity ownership to be credible evidence of their confidence in the firm's future earnings.[4] One limitation of the model is that it does not seem to apply to firm repurchases of stock held by outside stockholders.

A number of researchers, most notably Miller and Rock as well as John and Williams, have emphasized the fact that many announcements of capital structure change convey information about firm cash flows.[5] Specifically, since a firm's sources of funds must equal its uses of funds, security sales, which raise external funds, can have negative implications for the levels of alternative sources of funds, which most notably include the firm's current earnings. Likewise, security repurchases, which absorb internal funds, can have positive implications for current earnings. Miller and Rock argue that the market draws negative (or positive) inferences about the firm's current and future earnings based on announced revisions in a firm's need to raise external capital. This argument implicitly assumes that the magnitude of profitable investment opportunities is relatively stable. Thus, this theory predicts that security price reactions are negatively related to changes in the magnitude of external financing but are independent of the form that this financing takes (that is, independent of the type of securities issued).

Myers and Majluf have developed a theory that posits that managers tend to sell securities to outside investors when the market has overpriced the firm's securities, based on their superior information about the firm.[6] In this way, existing stockholders benefit from the raising of additional funds at above market prices. Aware of this tendency, the market revises downward its assessment of a security's value whenever an offering is announced. Since stock is most affected by firm-specific information, it is also the security most susceptible to market prices deviating from the manager's informed assessment. Convertible securities, followed by low-rated debt, are the other securities most likely to be mispriced.[7]

In short, the Myers-Majluf theory predicts that a security price adjustment is triggered by an opposite change in security supply, and the magnitude of this adjustment varies directly with the security's overall risk. An implication of this observation is that managers should prefer to use internal funds over external funds. If external financing is necessary, the issuance of less risky securities is preferred to the issuance of more risky securities, given the latter security's greater negative security price reaction.[8] Myers argues that these preferences can be generalized into what is commonly referred to as the "pecking order" hypothesis.[9] However, Noe offers some counterexamples to the assertion that this can be generalized from the Myers-Majluf model.[10]

In contrast to Jensen, the Myers-Majluf analysis implies that stockholders prefer more "free" cash flow or unencumbered internal funds so as to avoid the averse selection risk premium that external financing involves.[11] Krasker extends the Myers-Majluf analysis by generalizing the project investment decision to include a scale decision.[12] This extension implies that the manager must choose not only whether to issue securities but also how much to issue. He obtains the further prediction that larger security offerings have more negative effects.

Heinkel and Schwartz argue that managers signal their own assessment of a stock's value through their choice of stock flotation method.[13] In this theory, which ignores potential differences in flotation costs, standby rights offerings of stock imply the highest stock value, ordinary rights offerings imply an intermediate price, and underwritten offerings imply the lowest price. Even though underwritten offerings involve higher flotation costs, the rights offering choice involves significant penalties to a firm setting an unduly high offering price. This ordering reflects the fact that the costs of offering failure are directly borne by the firm in the case of rights, and the longer time required for a rights offering gives investors more time to evaluate the firm. Standby underwriters are assumed to be able to distinguish between rights offerings that are overpriced and those that are not. Thus, only if rights offerings are not overpriced will the issuer find it profitable to employ a standby underwriter.[14]

Recent theoretical work on asymmetric information demonstrates that several other forms of financing decisions can have implications for firm security prices. Harris and Raviv argue that a firm's optimal call policy for convertible debt involves forcing conversion when the stock's current price is high relative to manager's inside information regarding its value.[15] Rational investors, however, will recognize the implications of a call announcement, causing the stock's price to fall by the expected value of this adverse information. Interestingly, even taking this reaction into account, managers can still find calling the debt under this policy to be optimal. Intuitively, firms with favorable information have lower costs of forgoing an immediate forced conversion since voluntary conversion is likely later on, while the benefit of not forcing conversion is an increase in the current stock price due to investor's beliefs that such forbearance signals favorable information. Conversely, firms with unfavorable information choose to call because the future benefits of forcing bondholders to convert immediately, when they otherwise would not have done so, exceeds the costs of the resulting decrease in the current stock price.

Evidence on the Information Models of Capital Structure Change

The evidence concerning the predictions of these various asymmetric information theories is reasonably supportive. Most of the average announcement effects reported in Table 2–1 can be interpreted as consistent with the Ross model's leverage predictions.[16] Additional supportive evidence is found in Vermaelen's study, which formally tests whether announcements of issuer tender offers, leverage-increasing events, are associated with unanticipated increases in firms' earnings in subsequent years.[17] While there are weaknesses in Vermaelen's methodology, his evidence appears to show surprisingly large gains in earnings in the subsequent five years. Whether this result is due to (1) abnormally high earnings prior to the tender offers biasing expected post-offering earnings downward or (2) actual earnings gains is still uncertain.

A second body of evidence that is supportive of several asymmetric information models is based on studies of the simultaneous price reactions of a firm's actively traded securities to particular capital structure changes. Pinegar and Lease analyze the effects of preferred-for-common exchange offers on firm value.[18] The estimated changes in firm value are found on average to be in the same direction as the leverage change. Kalay and Shimrat study common stock and straight bond price reactions to announcements of seasoned equity offerings.[19] They report that both stock and bond price changes are significantly negative, which indicates that the cause of these reactions is not due primarily to wealth redistributions among security holders but instead reflects a fall in firm value. The evidence in these two studies also supports Ross's asymmetric information model.

A different form of evidence is derived from senior management's stock trading activities preceeding announcements of capital structure change. If managers have superior information about the firm's future earnings that causes them to adjust the firm's capital structure, then they have an incentive to change their portfolio positions in the firms' stock as well. Several researchers have studied insider trading around selected capital structure changes using the SEC's "Official Summary of Security Transactions and Holdings" data. Lee studies insider trading patterns around leverage increases.[20] He reports that there were significant net insider purchases of stock prior to leverage-increasing exchange offer announcements. Karpoff and Lee study insider trading surrounding announcements of new issues of common stock, convertible debt, and straight debt.[21] They report that there is statistically significant net selling of stock by insiders several months prior to the announcement of both common stock and convertible debt issues. Issuance of straight debt seems to induce no significant change in insider trading patterns. These results are consistent with the previously discussed evidence of average stock price reactions to these same capital structure change announcements.

Another avenue of inquiry that has uncovered evidence consistent with asymmetric information effects induced by capital structure change is reported by Lease, Masulis, Page, and Young and by Barclay and Smith.[22] In these two studies, it is argued that firm participation in the primary or secondary market for the firm's stock increases the adverse selection risk borne by individuals trading in these stocks, and especially that borne by the stocks' specialists. The specialists are hypothesized to react to this increased risk of loss by raising their bid-ask spreads. Both studies report evidence that capital structure announcements appear to be associated with increases in the bid-ask spreads of these firms' common stocks. In the first of these studies, a short-term rise in the average spread is found on the announcement of seasoned common stock offerings. In the second paper, a long-run rise in the average bid-ask spread is reported for firms announcing secondary market stock repurchase programs.

Leland and Pyle's prediction of a positive relation between management stock holdings and firm value is supported empirically by the evidence reported in several studies.[23] Downes and Heinkel as well as Ritter analyzed initial public offerings of stock and found that management share holdings act as a positive signal which increases stock price.[24] Announcements of combination primary-secondary offerings of common stock analyzed in Masulis and Korwar were found to elicit a substantially more negative market reaction when management is selling a portion of their existing shareholdings.[25]

Turning to the Myers and Majluf and Miller and Rock models, the observed signs of the average stock price reactions to announced investment, dividend, and financing decisions generally are consistent with implications of their models.[26] Table 7–1 presents a summary of this evidence. But looking carefully at the financing announcement evidence, the relative size of the observed price reactions are strikingly consistent with the "pecking order" prediction of Myers, and inconsistent with Miller and Rock's prediction that any form of external financing is an equally negative signal.[27] For example, Dann and Mikkelson report that the average stock price reaction to announcements of straight debt offerings is insignificantly different from zero, while convertible debt offerings have significantly negative effects.[28] Hansen and Crutchley separately analyzed the mean annual return on assets (ROA) for large industrial firms issuing common stock, convertible bonds, and nonconvertible bonds over the 1977–1982 period.[29] They find that over each of the subsequent four years the ROA declines significantly for the three groups of issuers, which is qualitatively consistent with Myers and Majluf and with Miller and Rock. Interestingly, the ROA declines most for common stock issuers, and declines least for nonconvertible bond issuers, which is consistent with Myers' pecking order hypothesis.[30]

Several additional studies present evidence from situations where the predictions of Myers and Majluf and of Miller and Rock differ, and find support for the Myers-Majluf model. Masulis and Korwar have reported that average announcement effects for dual offerings of common stock and straight debt are of the same magnitude as common stock offerings, even though the average size of the dual offerings is twice as great.[31] Eckbo analyzed stock price effects of announcements of debt offerings by offering size and rating level.[32] According to Myers and Majluf, lower rated bonds should exhibit more negative price effects; Miller and Rock predict that the larger issues will be more negative. Eckbo reports that the lower the rating class, the more negative the price effect, but he finds no significant relationship to size. The Myers-Majluf model also predicts that firms realize gains from building up financial slack through a retention of earnings rather than by paying them out as cash dividends. This prediction appears to be in line with the evidence of Kalay, who finds that firms frequently retain earnings substantially beyond that required by bond covenants.[33]

Asquith and Mullins as well as Masulis and Korwar report significantly negative regression coefficients for offering size in regressions of stock returns at the announcement dates of seasoned common stock offerings, which appears to be consistent with Krasker's extension of the Myers-Majluf model.[34] However, Barclay and Litzenberger, using transaction-by-transaction data, also find an average negative stock price reaction of 1.5 percent in the first fifteen minutes subsequent to a stock offering announcement over the 1981–1983 period, but they find no significant relationship between this announcement effect and the log of the offering's dollar value.[35] They interpret this to support a transaction cost explanation for the stock price drop, specifically that investors must be compensated for altering their portfolios to accommodate the firm's equity offering. Vora and Yoon as well as Wruck study private placement of seasoned common stock and uncover a small *positive* market reaction to these announcements.[36] Vora and Yoon interpret this evidence as supportive of a positive certification effect from having a sophisticated financial institution agree to purchase the stock after receiving inside information from the firm.

Table 7–1. Average Stock Price Reactions to Announcements of Changes in Sources and Uses of Funds

Type of Announcement	Sample Size	Two-Day Announcement Period Return*
Implied Increase in Corporate Cash Flow		
Common Stock repurchase		
Tender offers[a]	199	16.9
Masulis[b]		
Open market repurchases	182	3.6
Vermaelen[c]		
Targeted small holdings	15	1.6
Bradley and Wakeman[d]		
Going private transactions	81	30.0
DeAngelo, DeAngelo and Rice[e]		
Dividend increase		
Dividend initiation	160	3.7
Asquith and Mullins[f]		
Dividend increase[g]	177	1.4
Charest[h]		
Specially designated dividend	164	2.1
Brickley[i]		
Investment increase	510	1.0
McConnell and Muscarella[j]		
Implied Decrease in Corporate Cash Flow		
Security sales		
Common stock[k]	388	–3.3
Masulis and Korwar[l]		
Preferred stock[m]	294	0.1*
Linn and Pinegar[n]		
Convertible preferred	30	–1.4
Linn and Pinegar[n]		
Straight debt[o]	459	–0.2
Eckbo[p]		
Convertible debt[q]	234	–1.7
Janjigian[r]		
Dividend decrease	49	–3.8
Charest[h]		
Investment decrease	111	–1.1
McConnell and Muscarella[j]		

Table 7–1. Average Stock Price Reactions to Announcements of Changes in Sources and Uses of Funds (Continued)

Note: This table is similar to Smith's Table 3, except that it reports average two-day common stock abnormal returns and sample size for representative studies of major changes in corporate sources and uses of funds grouped by their cash flow implications. (See Clifford Smith, "Investment Banking and the Capital Acquisition Process," *Journal of Financial Economics 15* (1986): 3–29.) Implied changes in corporate cash flows are calculated assuming everything except cash flow and the announced policy variable are unchanged. The statistics reported for each category of capital structure are based on the studies with the largest sample sizes. (Unless otherwise noted, announcement period returns are significantly different from zero.)

*Interpreted by the authors as not significantly different from zero.

a. See also Larry Dann, "Common Stock Repurchases: An Analysis of Returns to Bondholders and Stockholders," *Journal of Financial Economics 9* (1981): 113–38, and Theo Vermaelen, "Common Stock Repurchases and Market Signalling," *Journal of Financial Economics 9* (1981): 139–83.

b. Ronald W. Masulis, "Stock Repurchase by Tender Offer: An Analysis of the Causes of Common Stock Price Changes," *Journal of Finance 35* (1980): 305–19.

c. See Vermaelen (in note a).

d. Michael Bradley and Lee M. Wakeman, "The Wealth Effects of Targeted Share Repurchases," *Journal of Financial Economics 11* (1983): 301–28.

e. Harry DeAngelo, Linda DeAngelo, and Edward M. Rice, "Going Private: Minority Freezeouts and Shareholder Wealth," *Journal of Law and Economics 27* (1984): 367–401.

f. Paul Asquith and David W. Mullins, "The Impact of Initiating Dividend Payments on Shareholder Wealth," *Journal of Business 56* (1983): 77–96.

g. Also see Joseph Aharony and Itzhak Swary, "Quarterly Dividend and Earnings Announcements and Stockholder's Returns: An Empirical Analysis," *Journal of Finance 39* (1980): 1–12.

h. Guy Charest, "Dividend Information, Stock Returns, and Market Efficiency— Part II," *Journal of Financial Economics 6* (1978): 297–330.

i. James Brickley, "Shareholder Wealth, Information Signalling and the Specially Designated Dividend: An Empirical Study," *Journal of Financial Economics 12* (1983): 103–14.

j. John J. McConnell and Chris J. Muscarella, "Corporate Capital Expenditure Decisions and the Market Value of the Firm," *Journal of Financial Economics 14* (1985): 399–422.

k. Offerings by industrial firms. Also see Asquith and Mullins (in note f) and Wayne Mikkelson and Megan Partch, "Valuation Effects of Security Offerings and the Issuance Process," *Journal of Financial Economics 15* (1986): 31–60.

l. Ronald W. Masulis and Ashok W. Korwar, "Seasoned Equity Offerings: An Empirical Investigation," *Journal of Financial Economics 15* (1986): 91–118.

m. See also Mikkelson and Partch (in note k).

Table 7–1. Average Stock Price Reactions to Announcements of Changes in Sources and Uses of Funds

n. Scott C. Linn and J. Michael Pinegar, "The Effect of Issuing Preferred Stock on Common and Preferred Stockholder Wealth," University of Iowa Working Paper, 1985.

o. Excludes mortgage bonds. Also see Larry Dann and Wayne H. Mikkelson, "Convertible Debt Issuance, Capital Structure Change, and Financing-Related Information: Some New Evidence," *Journal of Financial Economics* 13 (1984): 157–86, and Mikkelson and Partch (in note k).

p. Espen Eckbo, "Information Asymmetries and Valuation Effects of Corporate Debt Offerings," *Journal of Financial Economics* 15 (1986): 119–51.

q. Also see Dann and Mikkelson (in note o), Eckbo (in note p), and Mikkelson and Partch (in note k).

r. Vahan Janjigian, "The Leverage Changing Consequences of Convertible Debt Financing," *Financial Management* 16 (1987): 15–21.

While the predictive power of the Myers-Majluf model is impressive in a number of dimensions, it should be recognized that neither this model nor the Miller-Rock model predicts price effects for pure capital structure changes such as issuer exchange offers, recapitalizations, swaps, or forced conversions of convertible securities. These actions involve no changes in sources or uses of funds and thus have no direct cash flow implications. Nevertheless, significant price impacts have been documented by Masulis, McConnell and Schlarbaum, Mikkelson, Finnerty, Peavy and Scott, Rogers and Owers and by Pinegar and Lease at the time of these announcements.[37]

In the Myers-Majluf analysis, security repurchases reduce financial slack, which is a valuable asset lost to the firm. At the same time, a repurchase of securities undervalued in the market can benefit existing shareholders. The net effect is ambiguous. However, significant price gains are documented for stock repurchases and debt calls by Masulis, Dann, Vermaelen, and by Mikkelson.[38] Finally, Eckbo reports that announcements of mortgage offerings, a form of low-risk secured debt, have more negative stock price reactions than do those of other (presumably more risky) nonconvertible debt offerings.[39]

There is another body of evidence that does not appear to be consistent with any of the well-known signaling-information theories, namely, the reactions of nonconvertible debt prices to announcements of capital structure change. If capital structure changes are interpreted by the market as signals of changes in firm value, then there should be like changes in the prices of not only the firm's common stock but also its nonconvertible debt. Furthermore, the riskier the debt, the larger the price effect that should be observed.

There are a number of studies that document significant deviations from the prediction of like changes in the prices of a firm's common stock and nonconvertible debt. For example, Masulis finds opposite price reactions by firms' common stock and nonconvertible debt on the announcement of leverage changes.[40] Mikkelson reports that nonconvertible debt prices exhibit a relatively large positive return on the announcement of calls of convertible debt, while common stock returns are significantly negative.[41] A number of other studies have found no significant positive price reaction in firms' junior nonconvertible debt to announcements of stock repurchases (see both Masulis and Dann) even though large changes in stock prices are observed.[42] Korwar and Kalay and Shimrat studied the announcement effect of seasoned common stock offerings and found a statistically insignificant or an economically small price drop for the nonconvertible debt, even though the stock experienced a large and highly significant price drop.[43] In a separate study of a different leverage changing event, Handjincolaou and Kalay find that while common stock price changes are often large at the time of dividend change announcements, those of nonconvertible debt are insignificantly different from zero.[44] They fail to note that these dividend changes cause only small increases in leverage. Peavy and Scott analyze nonconvertible bond prices on the announcement of stock for (existing) debt swaps and find an insignificant positive announcement return, while the effect for common stock is significantly negative.[45]

The predictions of Heinkel and Schwartz's model appear to be at variance with several pieces of evidence reported in the Eckbo and Masulis study of stock offering flotation methods.[46] Stock price reactions to stock offerings, on average, are negative for both standby and firm commitment offerings and almost zero for pure rights offerings. Further, the negative correlation between offer premium and the stock price change around the offering date of pure rights is contrary to the positive correlation predicted by Heinkel and Schwartz. On the other hand, this evidence appears consistent with the Myers-Majluf model if rights generally are subscribed by current shareholders. In this case, the adverse selection effect should be absent in the case of rights.[47]

Support for Harris and Raviv's predictions of negative stock price reactions to call announcements and subsequent decreases in firm earnings is found in a study by Ofer and Natarajan.[48] They reconfirm the earlier result of Mikkelson that there is an immediate price drop on such an announcement.[49] They also report evidence of unexpected earnings decreases in the five years subsequent to the call announcement. Unfortunately, Ofer and Natarajan do not test whether or not the earnings of firms abstaining from forced conversions exhibited unexpectedly strong performance.

Overall, a wide range of empirical evidence supports the predictions of the previously discussed asymmetric information models of capital structure change. But where predictions differ, the Ross, Leland-Pyle and the Myers-Majluf models appear to be the most consistent with the data.[50] For example, firms' market values appear to be positively related to the size of their managements' stock holdings and to announcements of equity offerings associated with downward revisions in market expectations of firm future cash flows which, on average, are realized. However, even these models appear to be unable to explain the motivation for many forms of capital structure change documented in the extant literature.

8

Theory and Evidence on Subsidiary Capital Structure Decisions

A firm's capital structure comprises more than simply the liability structure of the parent firm. Capital structure also includes the makeup of the debt and equity claims of each of its separately incorporated subsidiaries. Just as there are conflicts of interest between debt holders and equity holders of a parent firm, there are also conflicts of interest between the claim holders of the subsidiary and those of the parent, in addition to the conflicts among the subsidiaries' various claim holders. In part, this conflict is a result of the legal separation of subsidiary assets and liabilities from those of the parent. Under U.S. corporate law, each affiliated corporation as well as the parent firm is viewed as a separate legal entity, so the creditors of one affiliate have no claim to the assets of another affiliate or the parent.[1] An important tax consideration is that if the parent does not own at least 80 percent of the subsidiary's stock, it cannot file a consolidated federal tax return, which separately subjects subsidiary earnings to corporate taxation.

Subsidiary capital structures also have important implications for the measurement of parent firms' leverage ratios from consolidated balance sheet figures. As Beranek has forcefully argued, parent firm's leverage, defined in book value terms, is often overstated to the extent that there is (1) minority stock in subsidiaries (which should be counted in total firm equity), and (2) subsidiary debt that is not guaranteed by the parent and is thus not a claim on the overall assets of the parent (so that subsidiary debt is frequently riskier than the parent's debt and hence more heavily discounted by the market).[2] This discussion illustrates the potential importance that subsidiary capital structures have for the determination of the parent's capital structure.

To assess the significance of the subsidiary capital structure decisions, researchers have examined the announcement effects of these decisions on firm stock prices. Ideally, we would like to have information as to the effects of pure subsidiary capital structure changes, such as subsidiary exchange offers or the creation or dissolution of separate subsidiaries. However, this evidence is yet to be examined. Fortunately, somewhat similar events have been studied by Schipper and Smith, namely equity carve-outs.[3] These actions represent the initial public sale of equity in a wholly owned subsidiary of a parent firm (a subsidiary "going public").[4]

Schipper and Smith present several reasons why equity carve-outs may be beneficial to the stockholders of the parent firm. First, if outside investors can better assess the value of a subsidiary's assets in place relative to those of its parent assets, then carve-outs can decrease the cost of raising equity capital for investment in the subsidiary under the asymmetric information problem explored by Myers and Majluf.[5] With better investor information, the subsidiary would be subject to a smaller information discount when selling stock and hence would have a lower cost of equity capital. Second, separation of parent and subsidiary increases the supply of and demand for information about the subsidiary. The readily observable market price for the subsidiary's stock can increase the likelihood of a sale of the entire subsidiary. Third, having a market for the subsidiary's stock allows its management to have compensation plans based on the subsidiary's market value. This improvement in managerial incentives can be very valuable if the subsidiary management has substantial discretion in making operating and capital expenditure decisions. Carve-outs also can impose additional agency costs on the firm resulting from the conflicts of interest between the stockholders and bondholders of the subsidiary and its parent, which can generate significant legal costs for the parent firm. There also can be negative information effects of the type considered by Myers and Majluf and by Miller and Rock when the subsidiary stock is sold.[6]

Schipper and Smith report that on the announcement of equity carve-outs, the stock prices of the parent firms exhibit a significant average gain.[7] They also find that in most cases voting control remains with the parent firm and that many of these carve-outs have a limited life, either because they are subsequently sold off or are reabsorbed by the parent. Indeed, the carve-out may have been effected to facilitate the ultimate sale of many of these subsidiaries or to enable the firm to fund subsidiary capital expenditure requirements with a cheaper form of equity financing.

Another major form of subsidiary capital structure change that has been examined is the spin-off. This action occurs when a parent corporation distributes its entire holdings of stock in a subsidiary to the parent's stockholders. This event has the effect of completing the separation of parent and subsidiary assets and liabilities. In studies of spin-off announcements by Hite and Owers, Schipper and Smith, and Copeland, Lemgruber, and Mayers, average stock returns were found to rise significantly at the time of the initial and subsequent announcements.[8]

There are several explanations for this pricing effect. In some cases, spin-offs allowed the relaxation of regulatory constraints on the firm's overall operation (due to the imposition on the parent of regulations that apply specifically to the subsidiary) or the realization of tax benefits that otherwise would have been unattainable. Copeland, Lemgruber, and Mayers find some evidence that these valuation effects are related to the extent that the spin-off is tax free. In other cases, Schipper and Smith argue that firms realized gains by eliminating subsidiary operations that were far afield from those of the parent. Presumably, this separation alleviated the added strains placed on management because of the breadth of knowledge required to supervise this specialized subsidiary adequately.

One piece of evidence consistent with the tax/regulatory hypothesis is that the announcement period stock returns are on average larger for the subset of stock where these tax or regulatory benefits are clearly observed. Further evidence supportive of this last hypothesis is that less than a quarter of the spun-off subsidiaries are in the same industries as their parents.

Overall, subsidiary capital structure decisions can be important to the parent firm for many reasons. They affect the parent's ability to file a consolidated tax return, they affect the leverage of the parent, and they create potential conflicts between security holders of the parent and the subsidiary. While little evidence is available on the effects of subsidiary capital structure changes, the limited evidence that does exist suggests that decisions to allow subsidiaries to "go public" through the sale of minority stock can be beneficial to parent stockholders. The potential benefits of these actions include the ability to offer subsidiary managers stock-based incentive contracts, determination of a market price for the subsidiaries' equity prior to divestiture, the ability to raise equity capital for the subsidiary more cheaply, and tax and regulatory benefits to legally separating parent and subsidiary operations. However, empirical evidence supporting these benefits is quite limited.

9

Relation of the Leverage Choice to the Characteristics of a Firm, Its Common Stock, and Its Industry

Empirical Findings

Having reviewed the major theories of capital structure, we turn to the evidence on the relative importance of various firm characteristics that are predicted to influence the capital structure decision. To assess the incremental impact of each of these variables, the relationships between them and firm leverage can be estimated by means of a multivariate regression model. This approach is taken in the recent studies by Bradley, Jarrell, and Kim, by Long and Malitz, and by Titman and Wessels.[1]

In the study by Bradley, Jarrel, and Kim, leverage is regressed against three explanatory variables: firm earnings volatility, the ratio of depreciation and investment tax credits to earnings, and the ratio of advertising and R&D expenditures to net sales. These variables proxy for the risk of bankruptcy, nondebt tax shields, and discretionary or nonsecurable assets. The previous theoretical analysis predicts that these three variables should all be negatively related to leverage.[2] Empirically, the first and last variables are found to be significantly negatively related, while the second variable is significantly positively related to leverage. This evidence appears to support the importance of bankruptcy costs and the Myers-Majluf asymmetric information model, but not the nondebt tax shield effect.[3]

Long and Malitz estimate a similar regression equation but include several additional explanatory variables—namely, capital expenditures, operating cash flow, the firm's systematic risk or beta, and firm-specific risk. These variables proxy for tangible assets, the availability of internal funds, operating risk, and the probability of bankruptcy. Their predicted relationships to leverage are positive for the first variable and negative for the remainder. Empirically, Long and Malitz find results similar to Bradley, Jarrell, and Kim for the first three variables, except that nondebt tax shields are found to be negatively (although not significantly) related to leverage. The remaining variables are found to be significantly related to leverage in the predicted direction with the exception of the significant positive coefficient for firm-specific risk.

Titman and Wessels employ a recently developed alternative estimation method called linear structural modeling to measure the relationships between various firm characteristics and leverage. The primary advantage of this technique is that it explicitly accommodates explanatory variables that are proxies for their theoretical counterparts. The basic idea is that a set of proxy variables are employed to extract an estimate of an underlying common factor that more accurately represents the theoretically specified explanatory variable. These extracted factors then become the explanatory variables in the final analysis.

The seven extracted factors in the Titman and Wessels analysis and the theories that they proxy are growth (Myers[4]); asset uniqueness (Titman[5]); nondebt tax shields (DeAngelo-Masulis[6]); tangible assets (Galai and Masulis, Myers, Scott, Titman[7]); size (based on the economies of scale found in Smith and in Warner[8]); profitability (Myers and Majluf[9]); and volatility (Castanias; Bradley, Jarrell, and Kim[10]). In addition, there is a dummy variable for manufacturers of machines and equipment, which is an additional proxy variable for asset uniqueness.

The parameter estimates for all the variables except tangible assets were found to be negatively related to firm leverage. However, only the parameter estimates for asset uniqueness, profitability, and the industry dummy were statistically significant at conventional levels. The major advantage of the Titman-Wessels approach is that the proxy nature of the explanatory variables (the extracted factors) is taken explicitly into account by the statistical procedure. The major limitation of this procedure is that it gives the researcher great discretion in choosing the indicator variables that are used to construct the extracted factors, without giving the reader much information as to the sensitivity of the results to these choices.[11]

While the evidence developed by these studies is helpful, it must be interpreted cautiously. If there is a significant level of interdependence in the investment and financing decisions, then these results can be misleading to the extent that they fail to control fully for the effects of difference in asset structures across firms on their leverage decisions.

The Relation of Leverage to Common Stock Risk and Expected Return

A firm's capital structure is predicted to have a number of important effects on the properties of its securities. For example, both a security's risk characteristics (beta and variance) and its expected return are predicted to be positively related to firm leverage. This feature was demonstrated in the case of common stock by Hamada assuming the validity of a standard asset pricing model (specifically the capital asset pricing model, CAPM) and default-free debt.[12] This relation was shown for both risky debt and common stock by Galai and Masulis, using option pricing theory.[13] The latter paper also shows that higher leverage causes both stock risk and expected return to be more volatile through an increase in a stock's price sensitivity (or elasticity) to changes in firm value.

Surprisingly, little empirical work has been undertaken to explore the importance of the above predictions. Hamada estimated the market risk for both the total assets and common stock of

304 firms, using a simple market model regression. He confirmed that stocks have risk levels that are considerably higher and more widely dispersed than the firms' assets. He found that a stock's risk is closely related to the firm's asset risk after adjusting the stock's risk measure for the firm's long-term leverage (regressing stock risk on firm asset risk cross-sectionally; the resulting R-squared values ranged from 0.96 to 0.98). Hamada also showed that within industries stock risk estimates are considerably more dispersed than are firm asset risk measures.

Ro, Zavgren, and Hsieh explore how stock betas and return variances change over the twenty-four months prior to a firm declaring bankruptcy.[14] They argue that leverage is likely to be substantially increasing over this period as equity value falls, so the stocks' risk would be predicted to rise. They find stock return variance to rise significantly over this entire period. They also report that stock betas, using a Dimson adjustment for nontrading, also rise significantly up to the last six months prior to the bankruptcy declaration.[15] While this evidence supports the earlier predictions, Ro et al. unfortunately do not report the magnitude of the average leverage change experienced by these bankrupt firms.

Weinstein expanded on this stock return evidence by analyzing the expected returns of a large sample of risky corporate debt issues.[16] He finds that their expected returns are positively related both to firm leverage and the firm's rate of return variance (or earnings variability), a result also predicted by the Galai-Masulis analysis.[17]

Christie tests the positive relationship between stock return variance and firm leverage predicted by the option pricing model.[18] He finds that stock return variance is positively and significantly related to leverage (measured as face value of debt to market value of equity). He also finds that this leverage-variance relationship explains much of the observed negative relationship between stock return variance and stock price.

DeJong and Collins studied the stability of stock risk measures.[19] They estimate the risk of common stock returns using four alternative variable parameter regression techniques. Firms with higher leverage are reported to have less stable equity risk using any of the four measures. They suggest that, in addition to reinforcing Hamada's early evidence, this finding may explain the reason for the observed instability in stock risk—namely, the general instability in firm leverage ratios over short periods of time, caused in part by stock price changes.

The preceding evidence has several implications. First, compared to regressing market index returns against firm common stock returns, more accurate estimates of equity costs of capital may be obtainable from leverage-adjusted estimates of firms' asset risk (with "market" indexes likewise adjusted). This suggestion reflects the potentially serious biases introduced by ignoring the leverage-induced nonstationarities in estimation of a firm's market risk. Second, since firm leverage decisions significantly affect a stock's risk level, stockholders may prefer more stable leverage policies if they have preferred portfolio risk levels and bear transaction costs to readjust these portfolios.

Industry Determinants of Leverage: A Case Study of Depository Institutions

The studies of Bowen, Daley, and Huber; Castanias; and Bradley, Jarrell, and Kim have found that a firm's leverage ratio is positively related to the average leverage ratio in its industry.[20] They also found that industry leverage ratios were negatively related to the frequency of bankruptcy filings and the ratio of noninterest deductions to earnings in the industry. In addition, Campbell found that stock price reactions to an announced leverage change were related to whether a firm's leverage was moving toward or away from the industry norm.[21] The evidence concerning industry leverage patterns is consistent with the effects of an optimal capital structure operating at the individual firm level, though it is far from definitive.

One means of expanding on the previous evidence is to study the determinants of leverage in an industry exhibiting extreme leverage choices. Some of the best examples of this situation are commercial banks and savings and loan associations, which typically have leverage ratios of 95 percent debt to assets or higher. Orgler and Taggart consider how the factors affecting capital structure decisions might be different for depository institutions than for other corporations.[22] They note that the debt of these institutions is primarily made up of deposit liabilities, which pay tax-exempt liquidity service flows at the personal level. This tax exemption implies a higher net tax advantage to debt for these institutions, holding everything else the same.

Depository institutions also experience a lower expected marginal bankruptcy cost at a given level of leverage than do other firms because of two factors. First, the probability of bankruptcy is lower because of subsidized deposit insurance, which, due to its risk insensitivity, implies that financially weaker institutions receive greater insurance subsidies. Second, because depository institution insolvencies are handled in an expedited manner by federal deposit insurance agencies rather than coming under bankruptcy court supervision, the actual costs of bankruptcy are lower.

In addition, depository institutions have relatively high proportions of tangible assets that can be used to secure creditors (primarily Federal Deposit Insurance Corporation (FDIC) and Federal Saving and Loan Insurance Corporation (FSLIC)), and this property helps lower the costs of insolvency.[23] This cost advantage is heightened by the small number of major claimants in these institutions, often only the deposit insurer, which lowers the agency costs associated with negotiating, monitoring, and enforcing the contracts between the institution's stockholders and debt holders. In sum, depository institutions' high leverage appears to be related to their lower expected marginal cost of bankruptcy and to the partial personal tax exemption on debt interest payments (that is, liquidity service flows) at the personal level.

The potential importance of regulation in effecting corporate financing decisions is illustrated in a study by Scott, Hempel, and Peavy.[24] In this study of stock market reactions to stock-for-debt swaps by bank holding companies, they report that, unlike swaps of industrial companies where significant negative price reactions are observed, for bank holding companies positive price reactions are recorded for swaps (though their small sample was not sufficient to yield statistical significance). Their explanation for this difference in market reactions is that, in the case of banks, government regulations mandating minimum equity capital levels frequently force banks into issuing equity through a debt/equity swap that management would not have otherwise approved (possibly because they considered the stock underpriced). Thus, the negative averse selection effect experienced by industrial companies voluntarily making swaps (which retire debt through equity issuance) should not generally occur in the case of banks. This evidence of differential impacts for regulated and unregulated firms strongly suggests that empirical studies of capital structure should control for the effects of regulation in their analysis.

10

Interdependencies among Dividend, Investment, and Financing Decisions

Investment and Financing Decisions: Theory and Evidence

One implication of the Myers-Majluf analysis is that internal funds are less costly than external funds.[1] Masulis and Trueman derived a similar prediction using a model of firm value maximization under personal and corporate taxes.[2] In that model, reinvestment of earnings is a cheaper source of funds because it defers taxable payouts to the firm's stockholders, rather than because of flotation cost savings or asymmetric information effects. The deferral of dividend payouts reduces the present value of stockholders' personal tax liabilities. This tax benefit implies that these shareholders (if they are in positive tax brackets) will require a lower rate of return on reinvested earnings, or internal funds relative to external funds.

An important implication of a difference in the costs of internal and external funds is that an interdependence between investment and financing decisions is induced. This property becomes clear when it is realized that internally financed investment projects require lower rates of return to be acceptable than do externally financed projects. As a consequence, when earnings rise, creating greater internal funds, firm investment also is likely to rise, especially if external funds are being replaced by internal funds. Dotan and Ravid as well as Dammon and Senbet formally derive models with interdependent investment and financing decisions, while Cooper and Franks analyze some conditions inducing such interdependence.[3] The empirical evidence on this issue of interdependence is more difficult to obtain.

Evidence consistent with this predicted interdependence has been found by several researchers. There appears to be substantial evidence that managers prefer to use internal financing over external financing. This preference was documented in a survey of interviews with the chief executive officers of major U.S. corporations by Donaldson.[4]

More direct evidence is obtained by McCabe and by Peterson and Benesh, who develop statistical models to test the significance of this predicted interdependence of investment and financing decisions.[5] McCabe develops a three-equation interdependent model of investment, dividends, and debt financing incorporating a lag for each dependent variable, where each of the equations is derived from the firm's fundamental cash flow constraint. He estimates these equations from annual data for 112 individual firms over the period 1966–1973 using a two-stage least squares regression. McCabe's regression estimates show that in the investment equation current dividends and current debt financing have positive and significant effects on the investment decision. In the debt equation, both current investment and dividend levels have significant positive signs.

Peterson and Benesh reestimated these relationships with a three-stage least squares regression technique using annual data for 534 firms over the more recent 1975–1979 period. They report that in their investment equation current debt financing has a significant positive effect, while the current dividend has a significant negative effect. In addition, both current investment and current dividends have significant positive effects in the debt equation. All of these reported results are consistent with the predicted interdependence of corporate investment, financing, and dividend decisions.[6]

Dividend and Financing Decisions: Theory and Evidence

Holding a firm's investment decision fixed, a firm's dividend and financing decisions are intimately wed by its cash flow constraint. This relationship requires that, given current earnings, a change in the level of external financing must be exactly offset by an equal and opposite change in dividends. Both John and Williams and Miller and Rock have developed signaling models that emphasize this cash flow constraint.[7] Further, John and Williams conjecture that dividend payments convey credible information about firm value and can be used to reduce the dilution effect of equity offerings.[8]

The 1986 Tax Reform Act, which taxes long-term capital gains at the same rate as ordinary income, should substantially weaken the distinction between stock repurchases and the payment of extraordinary dividends. This convergence in tax treatment highlights the close relationship between certain capital structure changes and cash dividend payments. However, it is important to recognize that dividend payments are generally much smaller in size and more predictable.

Kalay and Shimrat study the dividend behavior of firms making seasoned offerings of common stock.[9] They document that on average firms unexpectedly decrease cash dividends over the two years preceding the stock offering as well as in the year of the offering. Actual dividend payouts also are found to be relatively small for industrial firms in the two years prior to their stock offerings as well as in the offering years.

Kalay and Shimrat report that the proportion of firms issuing stock that also has a zero dividend is found not to differ from a randomly selected comparison sample. This evidence indicates that firms do not eliminate cash dividends in periods when common stock is being issued. In part, this finding may reflect the fact that there are substantial economies of scale in flotation costs, which implies that increasing an equity offering to fund a continued payment of cash dividends involves relatively small marginal costs while yielding the benefit of a credible signal to investors that firm prospects continue to be good. Whatever the reason, the evidence is not consistent with cash dividend changes being perfect substitutes for common stock offerings. This study also does not seem supportive of the John-Williams model where cash dividends are used to offset a portion of the equity offering effects.

11

Summary of the Evidence and Suggested Avenues of Future Research

This book has reviewed a large and diverse body of empirical and theoretical research relating to corporate capital structure decisions. These decisions include the choices not only of a firm's leverage but also of the composition and characteristics of a firm's various traded and nontraded claims. A rich set of theories has developed that explores the motivations for and impacts of these complex contract structures.

The evidence strongly supports the relevance of capital structure decisions for the valuation of firms and their securities. The determination of capital structure decisions appears to be strongly influenced by traditional considerations, such as taxes and bankruptcy costs. The evidence is generally supportive of models of capital structure that include corporate and personal taxes as well as various costs of bankruptcy and financial distress.

Capital structure decisions also appear to be influenced by the costs associated with potential and actual conflicts of interest among debt holders, equity holders, and managers, and with the information asymmetries between managers and a firm's security holders. Of the various models of these effects, the agency cost model of Jensen and Meckling and the asymmetric information model of Myers and Majluf appear to have the greatest predictive power.[1] In addition, there is evidence supporting the theoretical prediction that a firm's leverage choice directly affects its equity's risk characteristics and expected returns.

Recent theoretical work predicts a relationship between corporate financing and investment decisions. Such an interdependence between firm investment and financing decisions implies interdependencies between a firm's asset structure and capital structure. Interestingly, a wide array of evidence indicates that a firm's capital structure is influenced by various characteristics of its asset structure and vice versa. Support is found for leverage being negatively influenced by the total risk of the firm's assets. The size of particular debt instruments outstanding and the characteristics of the debt contract appear to be related to the firm's level of tangible assets, the extent of specialization of these assets, assets' rates of depreciation or service flow and expected profitability, other tax aspects associated with asset ownership, and the asset values' sensitivities to firm use and maintenance decisions. The debt maturity structure also may be influenced by the existence of debt in a firm's asset structure, if stockholders are concerned with hedging the effects of interest-rate uncertainty. In short, the theory and evidence on optimal capital structures seems to be uncovering significant interdependencies between firm investment and financing decisions, especially when the decisions are broadly defined to include the characteristics of debt contracts.

Many questions remain unanswered. On the theoretical level, more dynamic models of firm financing decisions are needed that capture the effects of flotation costs, as well as tax and information asymmetries. Our theories need to be enriched to capture a broader set of variables that appear to influence the firm's capital structure decision rather than merely a small subset. On an empirical level, to what extent can investors infer new information about a firm's expected cash flows and risk from its financing decisions? How do various features of a firm's securities and other contracts affect managerial incentives and firm operating efficiency? To what extent do the conflicts of interest between equity holders and a firm's employees, suppliers, and customers influence the firm's financing decisions? Why do firms issue preferred stock?

Why do so few firms issue income bonds or putable stock? How significant are flotation costs for corporate financing decisions? Are rights offerings indeed cheaper than underwritten offerings when all the differences in flotation costs are taken into account?

What is the extent of the interdependence of firm investment, financing, and dividend decisions? Why do stock prices react negatively to announcements of rights offerings in the United States, but positively in many European countries? How is it that risky debt securities tend to have insignificant price reactions to capital structure announcements, while stocks exhibit large price reactions? What new methodological approaches suggest themselves as a means of enhancing our understanding of a firm's capital structure decisions? For example, can tax-based capital structure theories be more rigorously tested using cross-country evidence where significant differences in tax structures are present? More generally, the existing tax, bankruptcy, agency and information-based models need to be developed further, and in some cases integrated, so that more precise predictions can be made and clearer comparisons across competing models will result. These are but a few of the challenges before us, awaiting the careful and determined researcher.

Notes

Note: All multiple citations are listed in order of their publication dates.

Chapter 1: Leverage Ratios and Financing Decisions

1. A number of more specialized reviews of the capital structure literature are available and have influenced my own perceptions of this wide body of work. The most notable of these reviews are the following: Varouj Aivazian and Stuart Turnbull, "Taxation and Capital Structure: A Selected Review," University of Toronto Working Paper, 1986. Alan Auerbach, "Taxation, Corporate Financial Policy and the Cost of Capital," *Journal of Economic Literature 21* (1983): 905–40. Robert S. Hamada and Myron S. Scholes, "Taxes and Corporate Financial Management" in Edward I. Altman and Marti G. Subrahmanyam, eds., *Recent Advances in Corporate Finance* (Homewood, Ill.: Richard D. Irwin, 1985). Michael C. Jensen and Clifford W. Smith, "Stockholder, Manager, and Creditor Interests: Applications of Agency Theory," in Edward Altman and Marti Subrahmanyam, eds., *Recent Advances in Corporate Finance* (Homewood, Ill.: Richard D. Irwin, 1985). Richard Lambert and David Larcker, "Executive Compensation, Corporate Decision Making and Shareholder Wealth: A Review of the Evidence," *Midland Corporate Finance Journal 2* (1985): 6–22. Stewart Myers, "The Capital Structure Puzzle,"

Journal of Finance 39 (1984): 575–92. Myron S. Scholes and Mark A. Wolfson, "Employee Compensation and Taxes: Links with Incentives and with Investment and Financing Decisions," Stanford University Working Paper, 1984. Clifford Smith, "Investment Banking and the Capital Acquisition Process," *Journal of Financial Economics* 15 (1986): 3–29.

2. I have not fully addressed the effects of dividend payouts on leverage or the influence of corporate control conflicts on financing decisions. Nor have the effects on financing decisions of the structure of voting rights and their distribution across outside shareholders, or the powers and makeup of the board of directors between outsiders and insiders been explored here. While these are interesting topics where important research is currently going on, they seem somewhat tangential to the major questions being addressed in this book.

3. Note that capital consumption allowances have been excluded as an internal source of funds since this does not represent an increase in corporate resources but only a transformation of physical capital into financial capital.

4. The exclusion of capital consumption allowances explains why these statistics differ from those of Taggart, who finds an increase in internal sources of funds. See Robert Taggart, Jr., "Secular Patterns in the Financing of U.S. Corporations," in Benjamin M. Friedman, ed., *Corporate Capital Structures in the United States* (Chicago: University of Chicago Press, 1985).

5. Avner Kalay and Adam Shimrat, "Firm Value and Seasoned Equity Issues: Price Pressure, Wealth Redistribution or Negative Information," New York University Working Paper, 1985.

6. Clifford Smith, "Alternative Methods for Raising Capital: Rights versus Underwritten Offerings," *Journal of Financial Economics* 5 (1977): 273–307. Espen Eckbo and Ronald W. Masulis, "Rights vs. Underwritten Stock Offerings: An Empirical Analysis," Southern Methodist University Working Paper, 1987.

7. Daniel M. Holland and Stewart C. Myers, "Trends in Corporate Profitability and Capital Costs," in R. Lindsay, ed., *The Nation's Needs: Three Studies* (New York: Committee for Economic Development, 1979).

8. Taggart, "Secular Patterns in Financing."

9. Gordon Donaldson, "Corporate Debt Capacity: A Study of Corporate Debt Policy and the Determination of Corporate Debt Capacity," Division of Research, Harvard School of Business Administration, Boston, 1961.

10. David S. Kidwell, M. Wayne Marr, and G. Rodney Thompson, "SEC Rule 415: The Ultimate Competitive Bid," *Journal of Financial and Quantitative Analysis* 19 (1984): 183–95. Sanjai Bhagat, M. Wayne Marr, and G. Rodney Thompson, "The Rule 415 Experiment: Equity Markets," *Journal of Finance* 40 (1985): 1385–1401.

11. Smith, "Alternative Methods for Raising Capital."

12. Sanjai Bhagat, "The Effect of Pre-Emptive Right Amendments on Shareholder Wealth," *Journal of Financial Economics* 12, (1983): 289–310. Richard L. Smith and Manjeet Dhatt, "Direct Equity Financing: A Resolution of a Paradox: A Comment," *Journal of Finance* 39 (1984): 1615–24. Robert S. Hansen and John M. Pinkerton, "Direct Equity Financing: A Resolution of a Paradox," *Journal of Finance* 37 (1982): 651–65.

13. Robert S. Hansen, "The Equity Financing Method Decision: Empirical Evidence from the Standby Underwritten Offering," Virginia Polytechnic Institute Working Paper, 1987.

14. Eckbo and Masulis, "Rights vs. Underwritten Stock Offerings."

15. Wayne Mikkelson and Megan Partch, "Valuation Effects of Security Offerings and the Issuance Process," *Journal of Financial Economics* 15 (1986): 31–60

16. Mikkelson and Partch (ibid.) also find a surprisingly large proportion of equity issues in their sample of firms.

17. Robert A. Taggart, Jr. "A Model of Corporate Financing Decisions," *Journal of Finance* (December 1977): 1467–84.

18. David Scott and Dana Johnson, "Financing Policies and Practices in Large Corporations," *Financial Management* 11, no. 2 (1982): 51–59.

19. Paul Marsh, "The Choice between Equity and Debt: An Empirical Study," *Journal of Finance* 37 (1982): 121–44.

20. Paul Asquith and David W. Mullins, "Equity Issues and Stock Price Dilution," *Journal of Financial Economics* 15 (1986): 61–89. Ronald W. Masulis and Ashok W. Korwar, "Seasoned Equity Offerings: An Empirical Investigation," *Journal of Financial Economics* 15 (1986): 91–118.

Chapter 2: Capital Structure Change and Its Relation to Firm Value

1. Recent evidence by Travlos indicates that bidder stock price reactions to takeover proposals is significantly different depending on the form of financing as argued in Masulis 1980. Nickolaos G. Travlos, "Corporate Takeover Bids, Methods of Payment and Bidding Firms' Stock Returns," *Journal of Finance* 42 (1987): 943–63; and Ronald W. Masulis, "The Effect of Capital Structure Change on Security Prices: A Study of Exchange Offers," *Journal of Financial Economics* 8 (1980): 139–77.

   Travlos finds takeovers financed by exchange offers of bidder common stock are associated on average with a negative 4.0+ two-day average return while takeovers financed with cash are associated with a positive 0.4 percent two-day average return. Implicitly the cash financing is presumed to be either from internal sources or from separate debt financing. Thus, the conflicting evidence of bidder stock gains or losses to takeover attempts appears to be due to a failure to take into account the differential effects of the alternative financing methods. This finding is further evidence supporting the negative effect of common stock issuance on existing stock.

2. Surprisingly, there have been no studies of the announcement effects of warrant issuance or the initiation of leasing agreements.

3. While offerings of debt are predicted to have a positive effect on firm value, some recent studies report insignificant stock price reactions to announcements of straight debt offerings. See Larry Dann and Wayne H. Mikkelson, "Convertible Debt Issuance, Capital Structure Change and Financing-Related Information: Some New Evidence," *Journal of Financial Economics* 13 (1984): 157–86; Espen Eckbo, "Information Asymmetries and Valuation Effects of Corporate Debt Offerings," *Journal of Financial Economics* 15 (1986): 119–51; and Wayne Mikkelson and Megan Partch, "Valuation Effects of Security Offerings and the Issuance Process," *Journal of Financial Economics* 15 (1986): 31–60. This finding may reflect a relatively high degree of predictability for debt offerings because often they are issued to replace maturing debt issues or short-term bank debt. In addition to these listed studies, Richard Dietrich ("Effects of Early Bond Refunding: An Empirical Investigation of Security Returns," *Journal of Accounting and*

Economics 6 [1984]: 67–96) investigates the effects of early bond refundings, in which little or no leverage change is occurring. On average, he finds no discernible stock price reactions to these announcements.

4. Ronald W. Masulis, "The Effect of Capital Structure Change on Security Prices"; also "The Impact of Capital Structure Change on Firm Value: Some Estimates," *Journal of Finance 38* (1983): 107–26.

5. Ronald W. Masulis, "Stock Repurchase by Tender Offer: An Analysis of the Causes of Common Stock Price Changes," *Journal of Finance 35* (1980): 305–19.

6. John J. McConnell and Gary G. Schlarbaum, "Evidence on the Impact of Exchange Offers on Security Prices: The Case of Income Bonds," *Journal of Business 54* (1981): 65–85.

7. Wayne Mikkelson, "Convertible Calls and Security Returns," *Journal of Financial Economics 9* (1981): 237–64, and "Capital Structure Change and Decreases in Stockholders' Wealth: A Cross-Sectional Study of Convertible Security Calls," in Benjamin M. Friedman, ed. *Corporate Capital Structures in the United States* (Chicago: University of Chicago Press, 1985).

8. Masulis and Korwar, "Seasoned Equity Offerings."

9. An example of an information effect observed in stock prices that is independent of any direct changes in capital structure or asset structure is the evidence of Mark Grinblatt, Ronald Masulis, and Sheridan Titman ("The Valuation Effects of Stock Splits and Stock Dividends," *Journal of Financial Economics 13* [1984]: 461–90), that stock splits and stock dividends that are announced independently of cash dividends have significant positive price effects.

10. Robert M. Bowen, Lane A. Daley, and Charles C. Huber, Jr., "Evidence on the Existence and Determinants of Inter-Industry Differences in Leverage," *Financial Management 11* (1982): 10–20. Richard Castanias, "Bankruptcy Risk and Optimal Capital Structure," *Journal of Finance 38* (1983): 1617–35. Michael Bradley, Greg Jarrell, and E. Han Kim, "On the Existence of an Optimal Capital Structure: Theory and Evidence," *Journal of Finance 39* (1984): 857–78.

11. Bowen, Daley, and Huber, "Existence and Determinants of Inter-Industry Differences in Leverage." John A. Boquist and William T. Moore ("Inter-Industry Leverage Differences and the DeAngelo-Masulis Tax Shield Hypothesis," *Financial Management* 13 [1984]: 5–9) report that this result is sensitive to whether leverage is defined in book value or market value terms. Bradley, Jarrell, and Kim ("On the Existence of an Optimal Capital Structure") also report evidence that does not appear to support this conclusion.

12. Castanias, "Bankruptcy Risk and Optimal Capital Structure."

13. Cynthia Campbell, "Industry Leverage Regularities: Optimal Capital Structures or Neutral Mutations?" University of Michigan Working Paper, 1986.

14. Most of these studies also suffer from an inability to control for the potentially important effects of asset structure differences on the firms' leverage decisions.

Chapter 3: Tax Effects of Capital Structure

1. Merton Miller, "Debt and Taxes," *Journal of Finance 32* (1977): 261–76.

2. Harry DeAngelo and Ronald W. Masulis, "Optimal Capital Structure under Corporate and Personal Taxation," *Journal of Financial Economics 8* (1980):3–30.

3. William Fung and Michael Theobald ("Dividends and Debt under Alternative Tax Systems," *Journal of Financial and Quantitative Analysis 9* [1984]: 59–72) extend the DeAngelo-Masulis analysis to the tax codes of Britain, France, and Germany, and conclude that the net tax advantage of debt in these countries is lower than in the United States, if positive at all.

4. Ronald W. Masulis, "The Impact of Capital Structure Change on Firm Value: Some Estimates." *Journal of Finance 38* (1983): 107–26.

5. Stephen Ross, "The Determination of Financial Structure: The Incentive-Signalling Approach," *Bell Journal of Economics 8* (1977): 23–40.

6. Alan Auerbach and Merwyn King, "Taxation, Portfolio Choice and the Debt-Equity Ratios: A General Equilibrium Model," *Quarterly Journal of Economics 97* (1983): 587–609.

7. Richard Green and Eli Talmor, "The Structure and Incentive Effects of Corporate Tax Liabilities," *Journal of Finance 40* (1985): 1095–1114.

8. Colin Mayer, "Corporation Tax, Finance and the Cost of Capital," *Review of Economic Studies 53* (1986): 93–112.

9. Brennan and Schwartz have explored some of the difficult problems associated with a multiperiod model of firm financing decisions under uncertainty. They incorporate corporate taxes, bond indenture restrictions, and the firm's sources and uses of funds constraint in a rational expectations equilibrium. Understandably, they are not able to incorporate more complicated tax structures that include personal taxes and are forced to assume a very stylized stochastic process for asset valuation. See Michael Brennan and Eduardo Schwartz, "Optimal Financial Policy and Firm Valuation," *Journal of Finance 39* (1984): 593–607.

10. Stephen Ross, "Debt and Taxes and Uncertainty," *Journal of Finance 40* (1985): 637–58.

11. Ross (ibid.) has developed a model of optimal capital structure focusing on the effects of firm cash flow uncertainty. He assumes a progressive tax code so that unanticipated increases in aggregate cash flows imply periods with higher marginal tax rates. Thus, he obtains the result that "In a cross section of firms with the same total variance, those with higher (positive) cash flow betas will have lower debt levels" (Theorem 7). While this is an interesting additional theoretical prediction, it has yet to be tested. Dammon also considers some further effects of a progressive personal tax code. Robert Dammon, "A Security Market and Capital Structure Equilibrium under Uncertainty with Progressive Personal Taxes," in A. Chen, ed., *Research in Finance*, vol. 7 (Greenwich, Conn.: JAI Press 1987).

12. Masulis, "The Impact of Capital Structure Change on Firm Value." Wayne Mikkelson, "Capital Structure Change and Decreases in Stockholders' Wealth: A Cross-Sectional Study of Convertible Security Calls," in Benjamin M. Friedman, ed., *Corporate Capital Structures in the United States* (Chicago: University of Chicago Press, 1985).

13. Jess Yawitz and James Anderson, "The Effect of Bond Refunding on Shareholder Wealth," *Journal of Finance 32* (1977): 1738–46. William Marshall and Jess Yawitz, "Optimal Terms of the Call Provision on a Corporate Bond," *Journal of Financial Research 3* (1980): 203–211.

14. W.M. Boyce and A.J. Kalotay, "Tax Differentials and Callable Bonds," *Journal of Finance 34* (1979): 825–38.

15. Joseph Cordes and Steven Sheffrin, "Taxation and the Sectoral Allocation of Capital in the U.S.," *National Tax Journal 34* (1981): 419–32.

16. Rosanne Altshuler and Alan Auerbach, "The Significance of Tax Law Asymmetries: An Empirical Investigation," National Bureau of Economic Research Working Papers, 1987.

17. Mayer, "Corporation Tax, Finance and the Cost of Capital."

18. Jack Mintz, "An Empirical Estimate of Corporate Tax Refundability and Effective Tax Rates," *Quarterly Journal of Economics 103* (1988): 225–31.

19. Alan J. Auerbach and James M. Poterba, "Tax Loss Carryforwards and Corporate Tax Incentives," in M. Feldstein, ed., *The Effects of Taxation on Capital Accummulation* (Chicago: University of Chicago Press, 1987), pp. 305–38.

20. Felicia Marston and Robert Harris, "Substitutability of Leases and Debt in Corporate Capital Structures," University of North Carolina Working Paper, 1986.

21. One inconsistent piece of evidence is a study by James Ang and Pamela Peterson which reports that leases and debt are positively correlated ("The Leasing Puzzle," *Journal of Finance 39* [1984]: 1055–65). It is noteworthy that this study examined only capitalized leases, ignoring the large role of noncapitalized leases documented by Marston and Harris ("Subtitutability of Leases and Debt in Corporate Capital Structures"). Ang and Peterson also employed book value of equity to scale the firm-specific variables rather than market value of equity. To the extent that this procedure introduces measurement error into both the dependent and explanatory variables, a positive correlation can be induced. Further research on this question is clearly needed.

22. Both Auerbach and Taggart present information concerning the changes in tax rates over this century. See Alan Auerbach, "Corporate Taxation in the United States," *Brookings Papers on Economic Activity* (1983): 451–505, and Robert A. Taggart, Jr., "Secular Patterns in the Financing of U.S. Corporations," in Benjamin M. Friedman, ed., *Corporate Capital Structures in the United States* (Chicago: University of Chicago Press, 1985).

23. John D. Finnerty, "Stock-for-Debt Swaps and Shareholder Returns," *Financial Management 14* (1985): 5–17. Ronald C. Rogers and James E. Owers, "Equity for Debt Exchanges and Stockholder Wealth," *Financial Management 14* (1985): 18–26.

24. For some statistics on the extent of this activity see Table 7 of "Analysis of Safe Harbor Leasing," Joint Committee on Taxation, 97th Cong., June 19, 1982.

25. Clyde Stickney, Roman Weil, and Mark Wolfson, "Income Taxes and Tax-Transfer Leases," *Accounting Review* (1983): 439–59.

26. Lambert Vanthienen and Theo Vermaelen, "The Relevance of Corporate and Personal Taxes for Financing Decisions and Security Pricing: Evidence from the 1982/83 Belgian Tax Reform," Catholic University of Leuven Working Paper, Belgium, 1985.

27. Espen Eckbo and Ronald W. Masulis, "Rights vs. Underwritten Stock Offerings: An Empirical Analysis," Southern Methodist University Working Paper, 1987. Paul Marsh, " Equity Rights Issues and the Efficiency of the UK Stock Market," *Journal of Finance* 34 (1979): 839–62. Claudio Loderer and Heinz Zimmerman, "Rights Issues in Switzerland: Some Findings to Consider in the Debate over Financing Decisions," Purdue University Working Paper, 1985.

28. Janette Rutterford, "An International Perspective on the Capital Structure Puzzle," *Midland Corporate Finance Journal* 3 (1985): 60–72.

29. For example, in Rutterford's Table 5 (ibid.) only data on average effective corporate tax rates inclusive of the effects of firm debt is reported. For a cross-country analysis of these different tax effects see Fung and Theobald "Dividends and Debt under Alternative Tax Systems."

30. Iraj Fooladi and Gordon Roberts, "On Preferred Stock Issued by Unregulated Firms in Different Countries," Dalhousie University Working Paper, 1986.

Chapter 4: Costs of Bankruptcy and Financial Distress

1. Richard Castanias, "Bankruptcy Risk and Optimal Capital Structures," *Journal of Finance 38* (1983): 1617–35. Richard Green and Eli Talmor, "The Structure and Incentive Effects of Corporate Tax Liabilities," *Journal of Finance 40* (1985): 1095–1114. Jayant Kale and Thomas Noe, "Business Risk, Optimal Debt Level, and Regulation: Should 'More Risky' Firms Have Less Debt?" Georgia State University Working Paper, January 1987.

2. Merton Miller, "Debt and Taxes," *Journal of Finance 32* (1977): 261–76.

3. Harry DeAngelo and Ronald W. Masulis, "Optimal Capital Structure Under Corporate and Personal Taxation," *Journal of Financial Economics 8* (1980): 3–30.

4. Sheridan Titman, "The Effect of Capital Structure on a Firm's Liquidation Decision," *Journal of Financial Economics 13* (1984): 137–51.

5. See "Harvester to Seek Supplier Concessions of $50 Million as Part of Financing Plan," *Wall Street Journal,* September 17, 1982.

6. Alan Shapiro and Sheridan Titman, "An Integrated Approach to Corporate Risk Management," *Midland Corporate Finance Journal 3* (1985): 41–56.

7. Jerold Warner, "Bankruptcy Costs: Some Evidence," *Journal of Finance 32* (1977): 337–47.

8. Edward Altman, "A Further Empirical Investigation of the Bankruptcy Cost Question," *Journal of Finance 39* (1984): 1067–89.

9. Altman also estimates these indirect costs by measuring the difference between security analysts' earning estimates and actual earnings of these firms prior to bankruptcy. Obviously, part of the difference is due to causes other than indirect bankruptcy costs, a point that Altman explicity recognizes but has no way to control.

10. Richard Castanias, "Bankruptcy Risk and the Optimal Capital Structure," *Journal of Finance 38* (1983): 1617–35.

11. Robert H. Litzenberger, "Some Observations on Capital Structure and the Impact of Recent Recapitalizations on Share Prices," *Journal of Financial and Quantitative Analysis 21* (1986): 59–71.

Chapter 5: Debt/Equity Agency Costs

1. Eugene F. Fama and Merton H. Miller, *The Theory of Finance* (New York: Holt, Rinehart and Winston, 1972). Dan Galai and Ronald W. Masulis, "The Option Pricing Model and the Risk Factor of Stock," *Journal of Financial Economics 3* (1976): 53–81. Michael C. Jensen and William H. Meckling, "Theory of the Firm: Managerial Behavior, Agency Costs and Ownership Structure," *Journal of Financial Economics 3* (1976): 305–60. Stewart Myers, "The Determinants of Corporate Borrowing," *Journal of Financial Economics 5* (1977): 147–75. Clifford Smith and Jerold Warner, "On Financial Contracting: An Analysis of Bond Covenants," *Journal of Financial Economics 7* (1979): 117–61.

2. Galai and Masulis, "The Option Pricing Model and the Risk Factor of Stock."

3. See the recent concern expressed about debt holders' losses in leverage buyouts, as exemplified by articles in the business press such as "Takeovers and Buyouts Clobber Blue-Chip Bondholders," *Business Week*, November 11, 1985, and "Not the Preferred Treatment—Proposed Uniroyal Buyout Hurts One Class of Securities," *Barron's*, June 17, 1985.

4. Fischer Black and John Cox ("Valuing Corporate Securities: Some Effects of Bond Indenture Provisions," *Journal of Finance 31* [1976]: 351–67) and Thomas Ho and Ronald F. Singer ("Bond Indenture Provisions and the Risk of Corporate Debt," *Journal of Financial Economics 10* [1982]: 375–406) apply option pricing theory to assess the incremental value gains to bonds and their changes in risk from introducing various bond indenture features.

5. Jensen and Meckling, "Theory of the Firm."

6. Myers, "The Determinants of Corporate Borrowing."

7. Smith and Warner, "On Financial Contracting." Richard C. Green, "Investment Incentives, Debt and Warrants," *Journal of Financial Economics 13* (1984): 115–36.

8. Zvi Bodie and Robert Taggart, "Future Investment Opportunities and the Value of the Call Provision on a Bond," *Journal of Finance 33* (1978): 1187–1200. Janet S. Thatcher, "The Choice of Call Provision Terms: Evidence of the Existence of Agency Costs of Debt," *Journal of Finance 40* (1985): 549–61. For additional analysis of

this problem, see Amir Barnea, Robert A. Haugen, and Lemma W. Senbet, "A Rationale for Debt Maturity Structure and Call Provisions in the Agency Theoretic Framework," *Journal of Finance* 35 (1980): 1223–34.

9. Rene M. Stulz and Herb Johnson, "An Analysis of Secured Debt," *Journal of Financial Economics* 14 (1985): 501–21.

10. Smith and Warner, "On Financial Contracting."

11. Stewart Myers and Nicholas Majluf, "Corporate Financing and Investment Decisions When Firms Have Information Investors Do Not Have," *Journal of Financial Economics* 13 (1984): 187–221.

12. Clifford Smith and L. MacDonald Wakeman, "Determinants of Corporate Leasing Policy," *Journal of Finance* 40 (1985): 895–908.

13. J. Michael Harrison and William F. Sharpe, "Optimal Funding and Asset Allocation Rules for Defined-Benefit Pension Plans," in Zvi Bodie and John Shoven, eds., *Financial Aspects of the U.S. Pension System*, (Chicago: University of Chicago Press, 1983). James Bicksler and Andrew Chen, "The Integration of Insurance and Taxes in Corporate Pension Strategy," *Journal of Finance* 40 (1985): 943–55.

14. Jerold Warner, "Bankruptcy, Absolute Priority and the Pricing of Risky Debt Claims," *Journal of Financial Economics* 4 (1977): 239–76. Ronald W. Masulis, "The Effect of Capital Structure Change on Security Prices: A Study of Exchange Offers," *Journal of Financial Economics* 8 (1980): 139–77.

15. Jeremy I. Bulow and John B. Shoven, "The Bankruptcy Decision," *Bell Journal of Economics* 14 (1978): 437–55.

16. Conflicts of interest between various groups of common stockholders can also occur. One cause of these conflicts is differential personal tax liabilities associated with firm security claims. For two manifestations of this conflict, see my 1980 study of issuer tender offers and my 1987 study, with Trueman, of investment and dividend decisions. Ronald W. Masulis, "Stock Repurchasing by Tender Offer: An Analysis of the Causes of Common Stock Price Changes," *Journal of Finance* 35 (1980): 305–19. Ronald W. Masulis and Brett Trueman, "Corporate Investment and Dividend Decisions under Differential Personal Taxation," *Journal of Financial and Quantitative Analysis* (1988) forthcoming.

17. Smith and Warner, "On Financial Contracting."

18. The evidence of Roberts and Viscione, who find that corporate bond coupons tend to fall with greater seniority and security, and Weinstein, who finds that corporate bond returns are positively related to firm leverage and the risk of default, is also consistent with this analysis. See Gordon S. Roberts and Jerry A. Viscione, "The Impact of Seniority and Security Covenants on Bond Yields: A Note," *Journal of Finance 39* (1984): 1597–1602, and Mark Weinstein, "Bond Systematic Risk and the Option Pricing Model," *Journal of Finance 38* (1983): 1415–29.

19. Morey W. McDaniel, "Bondholders and Corporate Governance," *The Business Lawyer 41* (1986): 413–60.

20. E. Han Kim, John McConnell, and Paul Greenwood, "Capital Structure Rearrangements and Me-First Rules in an Efficient Market," *Journal of Finance 32* (1977): 789–810. Ronald W. Masulis, "The Effect of Capital Structure Change on Security Prices: A Study of Exchange Offers." Robert H. Litzenberger, "Some Observations on Capital Structure and the Impact of Recent Recapitalizations on Share Prices," *Journal of Financial and Quantitative Analysis 21* (1986): 59–71.

21. Mikkelson reports evidence of capital structure changes that appear to benefit bondholders at the expense of stockholders. At the announcement of calls forcing conversion to stock of outstanding convertible debt, Mikkelson finds that the average stock price reaction is negative, while the average price change for the nonconvertible debt is strongly positive. Mikkelson interprets this to indicate that the holders of nonconvertible debt are benefiting from the lowering of firm leverage. See Wayne Mikkelson, "Convertible Calls and Security Returns," *Journal of Financial Economics 9* (1981): 237–64.

22. J. Michael Pinegar and Ronald C. Lease, "The Impact of Preferred-for-Common Exchange Offers on Firm Value," *Journal of Finance 41* (1986): 795–814. Masulis, "The Effect of Capital Structure Change on Security Prices."

23. Litzenberger, "Capital Structure and the Impact of Recent Recapitalizations on Share Prices." Two other case studies that find adverse wealth transfers borne by bondholders are Wansley and Fayez's study of stock repurchase by Teledyne and

Alexander, Benson, and Gunderson's study of TransWorld Corporation's spin-off of TWA. See James Wansley and Elayan Fayez, "Stock Repurchases and Security Holder Returns: A Case Study of Teledyne," *Journal of Financial Research* 9 (1986): 179–91, and Gordon Alexander, George Benson, and Elizabeth Gunderson, "Asset Redeployment: TransWorld Corporation's Spinoff of TWA," *Financial Management* (1986): 50–58.

24. Kenneth Lehn and Annette Poulsen, "Leveraged Buyouts: Wealth Created or Wealth Redistributed," Washington University Working Paper, 1987.

25. Masulis, "Stock Repurchase by Tender Offer." Larry Dann, "Common Stock Repurchases: An Analysis of Returns to Bondholders and Stockholders," *Journal of Financial Economics* 9 (1981): 113–38.

26. Wealth transfers that benefit debt holders at stockholders' expense are also possible, but less frequent (see note 21). Another example is defeasance of a debt issue, which effectively eliminates default risk but involves the continued payment to these investors of the higher risk interest rate that originally was compensation for bearing default risk.

27. David Mayers and Clifford Smith, "Ownership Structure and Control: The Mutualization of Stock Life Insurance Companies," *Journal of Financial Economics* 16 (1986): 73–98.

28. Smith and Wakeman ("Determinants of Corporate Leasing Policy") review the various advantages and disadvantages for leasing, including a careful analysis of the conflicts of interest between the lessor and lessee. They also develop a number of interesting predictions.

29. Thatcher, "The Choice of Call Provision Terms."

30. Espen Eckbo, "Information Asymmetries and Valuation Effects of Corporate Debt Offerings," *Journal of Financial Economics* 15 (1986): 119–51.

31. See U.S. Congress, Senate Committee on Labor and Public Welfare, "Interim Report of Activities of the Private Welfare and Pension Plan Study," 1971 (Washington, D.C.: U.S. Government Printing Office, 1972), pp. 85–86.

32. Martin Feldstein and Randall Morck, "Pension Funding Decisions, Interest Rate Assumptions, and Share Prices," in Zvi Bodie and John Shoven, eds., *Financial Aspects of the U.S. Pension System* (Chicago: University of Chicago Press, 1983). Zvi Bodie, Jay Light, Robert Morck, and Robert Taggart, "Funding and Asset Allocation in Corporate Pension Plans: An Empirical Investigation," in Zvi Bodie, John B. Shoven, and David A. Wise, eds., *Issues in Pension Economics* (Chicago: University of Chicago Press, 1987).

33. The continued risk of default on private pension liabilities and the sizeable underfunded liabilities that continue to exist are clearly documented in "Financial Status of the Pension Benefit Guaranty Corporation's Single Employer Insurance Program," Hearing before the Subcommittee on Oversight of the Committee on Ways and Means, U.S. House of Representatives, Ninety-eighth Cong., March 20, 1984 (pp. 36–44.) Washington, D.C.: 1984, U.S. Government Printing Office.

34. Martin Feldstein and Stephanie Seligman, "Pension Funding, Share Price and National Savings," *Journal of Finance 36* (1981): 801–24. Lane Daley, "The Valuation of Reported Pension Measures for Firms Sponsoring Defined Benefit Plans," *Accounting Review 59* (1984): 177–98. Wayne Landsman, "An Empirical Investigation of Pension Fund Property Rights," *Accounting Review 61* (1986): 662–91.

35. Bodie et al., "Funding and Asset Allocation in Corporate Pension Plans."

36. Fischer Black, "The Tax Consequences of Long-Run Pension Activity," *Financial Analysts Journal 36* (1980): 21–28. Irwin Tepper, "Taxation and Corporate Pension Funding Policy," *Journal of Finance 36* (1981): 1–13.

Chapter 6: Stockholder-Manager Conflicts of Interest

1. Michael C. Jensen and William H. Meckling, "Theory of the Firm: Managerial Behavior, Agency Costs and Ownership Structure," *Journal of Financial Economics* 3 (1976): 305–60.

2. A conflict of interest that can adversely affect a manager's wealth exists if the manager has invested in firm-specific skills. Then the value of that investment can be lost if a manager is fired by the stockholders. This threat makes the manager more sensitive to stockholders' interests but also discourages a manager from making this investment. Golden parachutes are one means of overcoming this manager-borne risk.

3. Harold Demsetz and Kenneth Lehn, "The Structure of Corporate Ownership: Causes and Consequences," *Journal of Political Economy* 93 (1985): 1155–77.

4. However, as firm size increases, limited wealth and decreased diversification make holding the same fraction of share ownership for monitoring purposes more costly.

5. Sanford Grossman and Oliver Hart, "Corporate Financial Structure and Managerial Incentives," in J. McCall, ed., *The Economics of Information and Uncertainty* (Chicago: University of Chicago Press, 1982).

6. Michael Jensen, "Agency Costs of Free Cash Flow, Corporate Finance, and Takeovers," *American Economic Review* 76 (1986): 323–29.

7. Eugene F. Fama, "Agency Problems and the Theory of the Firm," *Journal of Political Economy* 88 (1980): 288–98.

8. John Kensinger and John Martin, "Royalty Trusts, Master Partnerships and Other Organizational Means of 'Unfirming' the Firm," *Midland Corporate Finance Journal* (Summer 1986): 72–80.

9. Clifford Smith and Ross Watts, "Incentive and Tax Effects of Executive Compensation Plans," *Australian Journal of Management* 7 (1982): 139–57.

10. These contracts are forms of call options that have values that are positively related to the total risk of the underlying asset's value as shown by Black and Scholes. In the context of the stock option and stock appreciation right contracts, this underlying

asset is the firm's common stock. However, the stock itself can be viewed as a call option on the firm's total assets with an exercise price equal to the face value of the firm's debt. This observation implies that the stock's risk is determined by the risk of the firm's assets and the leverage of the firm. See Fischer Black and Myron Scholes, "The Pricing of Options and Corporate Liabilities," *Journal of Political Economy 81* (1973): 637–59.

11. Larry Dann and Harry DeAngelo, "Corporate Financial Policy and Corporate Control: A Study of Defensive Adjustments in Asset and Ownership Structure," *Journal of Financial Economics 20* (forthcoming 1988).

12. Michael Bradley and Lee M. Wakeman, "The Wealth Effects of Targeted Share Repurchases," *Journal of Financial Economics 11* (1983): 301–28. Dann and DeAngelo, "Corporate Financial Policy and Corporate Control." Paul Malatesta and Ralph Walkling, "Poison Pill Securities: Stockholder Wealth, Profitability and Ownership Structure," *Journal of Financial Economics 20* (forthcoming 1988).

Further evidence of management interest in ensuring its continued tenure can be found in studies of dual classes of voting stock by DeAngelo and DeAngelo and by Partch. See Harry DeAngelo and Linda DeAngelo, "Managerial Ownership of Voting Rights," *Journal of Financial Economics 14* (1985): 33–69, and Megan Partch, "The Creation of a Class of Limited Voting Common Stock and Shareholder Wealth," *Journal of Financial Economics 18* (1987): 313–39.

13. Guy Charest, "Dividend Information, Stock Returns, and Market Efficiency—Part II," *Journal of Financial Economics 6* (1978): 297–330. Joseph Aharony and Itzhak Swary, "Quarterly Dividend and Earnings Announcements and Stockholder's Returns: An Empirical Analysis," *Journal of Finance 39* (1980): 1–12.

14. Paul Asquith and David W. Mullins, "Equity Issues and Stock Price Dilution," *Journal of Financial Economics 15* (1986): 61–89.

15. Demsetz and Lehn, "The Structure of Corporate Ownership."

16. Karen Wruck, "Private Equity Financing," unpublished Ph.D. diss., University of Rochester, 1987.

17. Kevin J. Murphy, "Corporate Performance and Managerial Remuneration," *Journal of Accounting and Economics* 7 (1985): 11–42.

18. However, the latter proxy measure has some serious limitations, as review of the Jensen free cash flow argument clearly illustrates.

19. David Larcker, "Short-Term Compensation Contracts and Executive Decisions: The Case of Commercial Banks," *Journal of Financial and Quantitative Analysis* 22 (1987): 33–50.

20. David Larcker, "The Association Between Performance Plan Adoption and Corporate Capital Investment," *Journal of Accounting and Economics* 5 (1983): 3–30. Sanjai Bhagat, James A. Brickley, and Ronald C. Lease, "The Impact of Long-Range Managerial Compensation Plans on Shareholder Wealth," *Journal of Accounting and Economics* 7 (1985): 115–29.

    This market reaction alternatively could be interpreted as a positive signal concerning firm earnings, if boards of directors typically adopt such plans in periods when a firm is expected to do well.

21. Mark A. Wolfson, "Empirical Evidence of Incentive Problems and Their Mitigation in Oil and Gas Tax Shelter Programs," in John Pratt and Richard Zeckhauser, eds., *Asymmetric Information, the Agency Problem, and Modern Business* (Cambridge, Mass.: Harvard University Press, 1985).

22. Harry DeAngelo, Linda DeAngelo, and Edward M. Rice, "Going Private: Minority Freezeouts and Shareholder Wealth," *Journal of Law and Economics* 27 (1984): 367–401.

23. However, it may alternatively represent new positive information concerning the firm's earnings prospects that are known to management and are being revealed partially to the market by the going-private attempt.

24. "Congoleum Corporation," Harvard Business School Case Study, Harvard School of Business Administration, 1981.

25. David H. Downes and Robert Heinkel, "Signaling and the Valuation of Unseasoned New Issues," *Journal of Finance* 37 (1982): 1–10.

26. Ronald W. Masulis, "Changes in Ownership Structure: Conversions of Mutual Savings and Loans to Stock Charter," *Journal of Financial Economics 18* (1987): 29–59.

27. Harold Demsetz, "The Structure of Ownership and the Theory of the Firm," *Journal of Law and Economics 26* (1983): 375–90.

28. Randall Morck, Andrei Shleifer, and Robert Vishny, "Management Ownership and Corporate Performance: An Empirical Analysis," National Bureau of Economic Research Working Paper, 1986.

29. Downes and Heinkel, "Signaling and the Valuation of Unseasoned New Issues." Jay R. Ritter, "Signaling and the Valuation of Unseasoned New Issues: A Comment," *Journal of Finance 39* (1984): 1231–37.

30. Theo Vermaelen, "Repurchase Tender Offers, Signaling and Managerial Incentives," *Journal of Financial and Quantitative Analysis 19* (1984): 163–82.

31. Irwin Friend and Joel Hasbrouck, "Determinants of Capital Structure," in A. Chen, ed., *Research in Finance*, vol. 7 (Greenwich, Conn.: JAI Press 1987).

Chapter 7: Information Implicit in Capital Structure Adjustment Decisions

1. Stephen Ross, "The Determination of Financial Structure: The Incentive-Signaling Approach," *Bell Journal of Economics 8* (1977): 23–40.

2. For example, see Ross (ibid.); Robert Heinkel and Eduardo S. Schwartz, "Rights versus Underwritten Offerings: An Asymmetric Information Approach," *Journal of Finance 41* (1986): 1–18.

3. Hayne Leland and David Pyle, "Information Asymmetries, Financial Structure, and Financial Intermediation," *Journal of Finance 32* (1977): 371–87.

4. This is one of the few information models that incorporates risk aversion into the analysis.

5. Merton Miller and Kevin Rock, "Dividend Policy Under Asymmetric Information," *Journal of Finance 40* (1985): 1031–51. Kose John and Joseph Williams, "Dividends, Dilution, and Taxes: A Signalling Equilibrium," *Journal of Finance 40* (1985): 1053–70.

6. Stewart Myers and Nicholas Majluf, "Corporate Financing and Investment Decisions When Firms Have Information Investors Do Not Have," *Journal of Financial Economics 13* (1984): 187–221.

7. While Myers and Majluf claim that their results, which are shown to hold for firms with riskless debt and one class of equity, generalize to more complicated capital structures, this suggestion is not formally demonstrated.

8. The Myers-Majluf model does not explain when equity should be issued rather than debt, which is a limitation that Myers and Majluf recognize.

9. Stewart Myers, "The Capital Structure Puzzle," *Journal of Finance 39* (1984): 575–92.

10. Thomas Noe, "Financing Hierarchies and Announcement Effects under Information Asymmetry," unpublished Ph.D. diss. (3rd essay), University of Texas at Austin, 1987.

11. Michael Jensen, "Agency Costs of Free Cash Flow, Corporate Finance, and Turnovers," *American Economic Review 76* (1986): 323–29.

12. William Krasker, "Stock Price Movements in Response to Stock Issues under Asymmetric Information," *Journal of Finance 41* (1986): 93–105.

13. Heinkel and Schwartz, "Rights versus Underwritten Offerings."

14. An alternative information mechanism which could be used to create a separating equilibrium is certification, an issue raised by Kip Viscusi ("A Note on 'Lemons' Markets with Quality Certification," *Bell Journal of Economics* [1978]: 277–79). This certification concept has been applied to investment banking by Sheridan Titman and Brett Trueman ("Information Quality and the Valuation of New Issues, *Journal of Accounting and Economics 8* [1986]: 159–72). They argued that if there are quality differences in investment bankers' ability to evaluate an issue, then higher quality issuers can indicate their higher value by choosing the higher quality investment banker.

15. Milton Harris and Artur Raviv, "A Sequential Signalling Model of Convertible Debt Call Policy," *Journal of Finance 40* (1985): 1263–81.

16. Ross, "The Determination of Financial Structure."

17. Theo Vermaelen, "Common Stock Repurchases and Market Signalling," *Journal of Financial Economics 9* (1981): 139–83.

18. J. Michael Pinegar and Ronald C. Lease, "The Impact of Preferred-for-Common Exchange Offers on Firm Value," *Journal of Finance 41* (1986): 795–814.

19. Avner Kalay and Adam Shimrat, "On the Payment of Equity Financed Dividends," New York University Working Paper, 1986.

20. Won Lee, "The Effect of Exchange Offers and Stock Swaps on Equity Risk and Shareholders' Wealth: A Signalling Model Approach," unpublished Ph.D. diss., UCLA, 1987.

21. Jonathon Karpoff and Daniel Lee, "Insider Trading Around Announcements of New Security Issues: Evidence of Information Signalling," University of Washington Working Paper, 1987.

22. Ronald Lease, Ronald Masulis, John Page, and David Young, "Market Reaction to Seasoned Equity Issues: The Impact of

Asymmetric Information," Southern Methodist University Working Paper, 1987. Michael Barclay and Clifford Smith, "Corporate Payout Policy: Cash Dividends versus Open-Market Share Repurchases," University of Rochester Working Paper, 1987.

23. Leland and Pyle, "Information Asymmetries, Financial Structure, and Financial Intermediation."

24. David H. Downes and Robert Heinkel, "Signalling and the Valuation of Unseasoned New Issues," *Journal of Finance 37* (1982): 1–10. Jay R. Ritter, "Signalling and the Valuation of Unseasoned New Issues: A Comment," *Journal of Finance 39* (1984): 1231–37.

25. Ronald W. Masulis and Ashok W. Korwar, "Seasoned Equity Offerings: An Empirical Investigation," *Journal of Financial Economics 15* (1986): 91–118.

    Vermaelen develops a signaling model where offer premium and fractional share ownership by management act as positive signals of firm value. He finds that market reactions to announcements of issuer tender offers are positively correlated to both offer premiums and changes in management's share holdings. Unfortunately, Vermaelen did not separately analyze tender offers excluding managers from those that do not. This would be a more convincing test since changes in management's share holdings are generally highly correlated with the size of the tender offer. See Theo Vermaelen, "Repurchase Tender Offers, Signaling and Managerial Incentives," *Journal of Financial and Quantitative Analysis 19* (1984): 163–82.

26. Myers and Majluf, "Corporate Financing and Investment Decisions When Firms Have Information Investors Do Not Have." Miller and Rock, "Dividend Policy Under Asymmetric Information."

27. Myers, "The Capital Structure Puzzle." Miller and Rock, "Dividend Policy Under Asymmetric Information."

28. Larry Dann and Wayne H. Mikkelson, "Convertible Debt Issuance, Capital Structure Change and Financing-Related Information: Some New Evidence," *Journal of Financial Economics 13* (1984): 157–86.

29. Robert S. Hansen and Claire Crutchley, "Corporate Financings and Corporate Earnings: A Test of the Miller-Rock Hypothesis," Virginia Polytechnic Institute Working Paper, 1986.

30. Myers, "The Capital Structure Puzzle."

31. Masulis and Korwar, "Seasoned Equity Offerings."

32. Espen Eckbo, "Information Asymmetries and Valuation Effects of Corporate Debt Offerings," *Journal of Financial Economics 15* (1986): 119–51.

33. Avner Kalay, "Stockholder-Bondholder Conflict and Dividend Constraints," *Journal of Financial Economics 10* (1982): 211–33.

34. Paul Asquith and David W. Mullins, "Equity Issues and Stock Price Dilution," *Journal of Financial Economics 15* (1986): 61–89. Masulis and Korwar, "Seasoned Equity Offerings." Krasker, "Stock Price Movements in Response to Stock Issues Under Asymmetric Information."

35. Micheal J. Barclay and Robert H. Litzenberger, "Intraday Market Reactions to Public Offerings of Corporate Securities," Standford University Working Paper, 1986.

36. Gautam Vora and Seung Jin Yoon, "Price Impact of Private Placement of Common Stocks: A Signaling Approach to Capital Market Efficiency," Pennsylvania State University Working Paper, 1986. Karen Wruck, "Private Equity Financing," unpublished Ph.D. diss., University of Rochester, 1987.

37. Ronald W. Masulis, "The Effect of Capital Structure Change on Security Prices: A Study of Exchange Offers," *Journal of Financial Economics* (1980): 139–77; "The Impact of Capital Structure Change on Firm Value: Some Estimates," *Journal of Finance 38* (1983): 107–26. John J. McConnell and Gary G. Schlarbaum, "Evidence on the Impact of Exchange Offers on Security Prices: The Case of Income Bonds," *Journal of Business 54* (1981): 65–85. Wayne Mikkelson, "Convertible Calls and Security Returns," *Journal of Financial Economics 9* (1981): 237–64; "Capital Structure Change and Decreases in Stockholders' Wealth: A Cross-Sectional Study of Convertible Security Calls," in Benjamin M. Friedman, ed., *Corporate Capital Structures in the United States* (Chicago: University of Chicago Press, 1985). John D. Finnerty, "Stock-for-Debt Swaps and Shareholder Returns," *Financial Management 14* (1985): 5–17. John W. Peavy and Jonathan A. Scott, "The Effect of Stock-for-Debt Swaps on Security Returns," *Financial Review 20* (1985): 303–27. Ronald C. Rogers and James E. Owers, "Equity for Debt Exchanges and Stockholder Wealth,"

Financial Management 14 (1985): 18–26. J. Michael Pinegar and Ronald C. Lease, "The Impact of Preferred-for-Common Exchange Offers on Firm Value," *Journal of Finance 41* (1986): 795–814.

38. Ronald W. Masulis, "Stock Repurchase by Tender Offer: An Analysis of the Causes of Common Stock Price Changes," *Journal of Finance 35* (1980): 305–19. Larry Dann, "Common Stock Repurchases: An Analysis of Returns to Bondholders and Stockholders," *Journal of Financial Economics 9* (1981): 113–38. Vermaelen, "Common Stock Repurchases and Market Signaling." Mikkelson, "Convertible Calls and Security Returns"; "Capital Structure Change and Decreases in Stockholders' Wealth."

39. Espen Eckbo, "Information Asymmetries and Valuation Effects of Corporate Debt Offerings," *Journal of Financial Economics 15* (1986): 119–51. However, there should be controls for other differences in offering characteristics that could exist in these samples.

40. Masulis, "The Effects of Capital Structure Change on Security Prices."

41. Mikkelson, "Convertible Calls and Security Returns."

42. Masulis, "The Effect of Capital Structure Change on Security Prices." Dann, "Common Stock Repurchases."

43. Ashok Korwar, "The Effect of New Issues of Equity," Ph.D. diss., University of California at Los Angeles, 1982. Avner Kalay and Adam Shimrat, "Firm Value and Seasoned Equity Issues: Price Pressure, Wealth Redistribution or Negative Information," *Journal of Financial Economics 19* (1987): 109–26.

44. George Handjinicolaou and Avner Kalay, "Wealth Redistributions or Changes in Firm Value: An Analysis of Returns to the Bondholders and to the Stockholders around Dividend Announcements," *Journal of Financial Economics 13* (1984): 35–63.

45. Peavy and Scott, "The Effect of Stock-for-Debt Swaps on Security Returns."

46. Heinkel and Schwartz, "Rights versus Underwritten Offerings." Espen Eckbo and Ronald W. Masulis, "Rights vs. Underwritten Stock Offerings: An Empirical Analysis," Southern Methodist University Working Paper, 1987.

47. Myers and Majluf, "Corporate Financing and Investment Decisions."

48. Harris and Raviv, "A Sequential Signaling Model of Convertible Debt Call Policy." Aharon Ofer and Ashok Natarajan, "Convertible Call Policies: An Empirical Analysis of an Information-Signaling Hypothesis," *Journal of Financial Economics 19* (1987): 69–90.

49. Mikkelson, "Convertible Calls and Security Returns."

50. Leland and Pyle, "Information Asymmetries, Financial Structure, and Financial Intermediation." Ross, "The Determination of Capital Structure." Myers and Majluf, "Corporate Financing and Investment Decisions."

Chapter 8: Theory and Evidence on Subsidiary Capital Structure Decisions

1. For further amplification on the legal issues surrounding the liability of the parent for the debt of its subsidiary, see Richard Posner, "The Rights of Creditors of Affiliated Corporations," *University of Chicago Law Review* 43 (1976): 499–526.

2. William Beranek, "Financial Disclosure, Asymmetric Information and Financial Risk Assessment," in Thomas Copeland, ed., *Modern Finance and Industrial Economics Essays in Honor of J. Fred Weston* (London: Basil Blackwell, 1986).

3. Katherine Schipper and Abbie Smith, "A Comparison of Equity Carve-Outs and Equity Offerings: Share Price Effects and Corporate Restructuring," *Journal of Financial Economics* 15 (1986): 153–86.

4. Another example of a major subsidiary capital structure change is divisional buyouts by their own managements. For an analysis of this phenomenon, see Gailen Hite and Michael Vetsuypens, "Management Buyouts of Divisions and Shareholder Wealth," Southern Methodist University Working Paper, 1988.

5. Stewart Myers and Nicholas Majluf, "Corporate Financing and Investment Decisions When Firms Have Information Investors Do Not Have," *Journal of Financial Economics* 13 (1984): 187–221.

6. Merton Miller and Kevin Rock, "Dividend Policy Under Asymmetric Information," *Journal of Finance* 40 (1985):1031–51.

7. Schipper and Smith, "A Comparison of Equity Carve-Outs and Equity Offerings."

8. Gailen L. Hite and James E. Owers, "Security Price Reactions around Corporate Spin-Off Announcements," *Journal of Financial Economics* 12 (1983): 407–33. Katherine Schipper and Abbie Smith, "Effects of Recontracting on Shareholder Wealth: The Case of Voluntary Spin-offs," *Journal of Financial Economics* 12 (1983): 434–66. Thomas Copeland, Eduardo Lemgruber, and David Mayers, "Corporate Spinoffs, Multiple Announcement and Ex-Date Abnormal Performance," in Thomas Copeland, ed.,

Modern Finance and Industrial Economics (London: Basil Blackwell, 1986). Copeland, Lemgruber, and Mayers report 11 percent of announced spin-offs are never completed. Thus, secondary announcements that increase the probability that the spin-off will be implemented should be considered in assessing the full economic impact of these actions.

Chapter 9: Relation of the Leverage Choice to the Characteristics of a Firm, Its Common Stock, and Its Industry

1. Michael Bradley, Greg Jarrell, and E. Han Kim, "On the Existence of an Optimal Capital Structure: Theory and Evidence," *Journal of Finance 39* (1984): 857-78. Michael Long and Ileen Malitz, "Investment Patterns and Financial Leverage," in B. Friedman, ed., *Corporate Capital Structure in the United States* (Chicago: University of Chicago Press, 1985). Sheridan Titman and Roberto Wessels, "The Determinants of Capital Structure Choice," *Journal of Finance 43* (1988): 1-20.

2. There are several reasons why managers may alter a firm's total risk that may have a bearing on the observed patterns of firm risk. Smith and Stulz mention three major motivations for hedging this risk: to lower expected bankruptcy costs, to increase expected value of net tax shields by minimizing the frequency of excess shields, and managerial risk aversion (combined with a compensation scheme that is heavily weighted toward a fixed payoff contract). See Clifford Smith and Rene Stulz, "The Determinants of Firms' Hedging Policies," *Journal of Financial and Quantitative Analysis 20* (1985): 391-405.

3. Stewart Myers and Nicholas Majluf, "Corporate Financing and Investment Decisions When Firms Have Information Investors Do Not Have," *Journal of Financial Economics 13* (1984): 187-221.

4. Stewart Myers, "The Determinants of Corporate Borrowing," *Journal of Financial Economics 5* (1977) : 147-75.

5. Sheridan Titman, "The Effect of Capital Structure on a Firm's Liquidation Decision," *Journal of Financial Economics 13* (1984): 137-51.

6. Harry DeAngelo and Ronald W. Masulis, "Optimal Capital Structure Under Corporate and Personal Taxation," *Journal of Financial Economics 8* (1980): 3-30.

7. Dan Galai and Ronald W. Masulis, "The Option Pricing Model and the Risk Factor of Stock," *Journal of Financial Economics 3*

(1976): 53–81. Myers, "The Determinants of Corporate Borrowing." James Scott, "Bankruptcy, Secured Debt, and Optimal Capital Structure," *Journal of Finance 32* (1977): 1–20. Titman, "The Effect of Capital Structure on a Firm's Liquidation Decision."

8. Clifford Smith, "Alternative Methods for Raising Capital: Rights versus Underwritten Offerings," *Journal of Financial Economics 5* (1977): 273–307. Jerold Warner, "Bankruptcy Costs: Some Evidence," *Journal of Finance 32* (1977): 337–47.

9. Myers and Majluf, "Corporate Financing and Investment Decisions When Firms Have Information Investors Do Not Have."

10. Richard Castanias, "Bankruptcy Risk and Optimal Capital Structure," *Journal of Finance 38* (1983): 1617–35. Bradley, Jarrell, and Kim, "On the Existence of an Optimal Capital Structure."

11. An example of this problem involves the construction of the asset uniqueness factor that is derived from several indicator variables, including research and development and advertising expense. These variables could be included as indicator variables for nondebt tax shields, but they are not in this study.

12. Robert S. Hamada, "The Effect of the Firm's Capital Structure on the Systematic Risk of Common Stock," *Journal of Finance 27* (1972):435–52.

13. Dan Galai and Ronald W. Masulis, "The Option Pricing Model and the Risk Factor of Stock," *Journal of Financial Economics 3* (1976): 53–81.

14. Byuno Ro, Christine Zavgren and Su-Jane Hsieh, "The Effects of Bankruptcy on Systematic Risk: An Empirical Assessment," Purdue University Working Paper, 1986.

15. Elwood Dimson, "Risk Measurement When Shares Are Subject to Infrequent Trading," *Journal of Financial Economics 7* (1979): 197–226.

16. Mark Weinstein, "Bond Systematic Risk and the Option Pricing Model," *Journal of Finance 38* (1983): 1415–29.

17. Roberts and Viscione present some further supportive evidence on the relation between security leverage and expected returns. They compare yields on sets of nonconvertible bonds having

differing seniority and protective covenants which are issued by the same firms. They find that debt with lower seniority or less restrictive protective covenants exhibit significantly higher yields. See Gordon S. Roberts and Jerry A. Viscione, "The Impact of Seniority and Security Covenants on Bond Yields: A Note," *Journal of Finance* 39 (1984): 1597–1602.

18. Andrew Christie, "The Stochastic Behavior of Common Stock Variances: Value, Leverage and Interest Rate Effects," *Journal of Financial Economics* 10 (1982): 407–32.

19. Douglas DeJong and Daniel Collins, "Explanations for the Instability of Equity Beta: Risk-Free Rate Changes and Leverage Effects," *Journal of Financial and Quantitative Analysis* 20 (1985): 73–94.

20. Robert M. Bowen, Lane A. Daley, and Charles C. Huber, Jr., " Evidence on the Existence and Determinants of Inter-Industry Differences in Leverage," *Financial Management* 11 (1982): 10–20. Richard Castanias, "Bankruptcy Risk and Optimal Capital Structure," *Journal of Finance* 38 (1983): 1617–35. Michael Bradley, Greg Jarrell, and E. Han Kim, "On the Existence of an Optimal Capital Structure: Theory and Evidence," *Journal of Finance* 39 (1984): 857–78.

21. Cynthia Campbell, "Industry Leverage Regularities: Optimal Capital Structures or Neutral Mutations?" University of Michigan Working Paper, 1986.

22. Yair E. Orgler and Robert A. Taggart, Jr., "Implications of Corporate Capital Structure Theory for Banking Institutions," *Journal of Money, Credit, and Banking* 15 (1983): 212–21.

23. These institutions also have a feature that increases their probability of bankruptcy, namely the fact that most of their debt is effectively short-term because of the put options written on deposits, which give holders the right of immediate redemption. This feature is, however, offset by Federal Reserve System and Federal Home Loan Bank System loans made available over the short run at subsidized rates to replace unexpected deposit withdrawals.

24. Jonathan A. Scott, George H. Hempel, and John W. Peavy III, "The Effect of Stock-for-Debt Swaps on Bank Holding Companies," *Journal of Banking and Finance* 9 (1985): 233–51.

Chapter 10: Interdependencies among Dividend, Investment, and Financing Decisions

1. Stewart Myers and Nicholas Majluf, "Corporate Financing and Investment Decisions When Firms Have Information Investors Do Not Have," *Journal of Financial Economics* 13 (1984): 187–221.

2. Ronald W. Masulis and Brett Trueman, "Corporate Investment and Dividend Decisions Under Differential Personal Taxation," *Journal of Financial and Quantitative Analysis* 23 (1988) forthcoming.

3. Amihud Dotan and S. Abraham Ravid, "On the Interaction of Real and Financial Decisions of the Firm Under Uncertainty," *Journal of Finance* 40 (1985): 501–17. Robert Dammon and Lemma Senbet, "The Effect of Taxes and Depreciation on Corporate Investment and Financial Leverage," *Journal of Finance* 43 (1988): 357–73. Ian Cooper and Julian Franks, "The Interaction of Financing and Investment Decisions When the Firm Has Unused Tax Credits," *Journal of Finance* 38 (1983): 571–83.

4. Gordon Donaldson, *Corporate Debt Capacity: A Study of Corporate Debt Policy and the Determination of Corporate Debt Capacity* (Boston: Division of Research, Harvard School of Business Administration, 1961).

5. George McCabe, "The Empirical Relationship Between Investment and Financing: A New Look," *Journal of Financial and Quantitative Analysis* 14 (1979): 119–35. Pamela Peterson and Gary Benesh, "A Reexamination of the Empirical Relationship Between Investment and Financing Decisions," *Journal of Financial and Quantitative Analysis* 18 (1983): 439–53.

6. This conclusion is still controversial, given the contradictory evidence of Eugene F. Fama ("The Empirical Relation Between the Dividend and Investment Decisions of Firms," *American Economic Review* 64 [1974]: 304–18) and of Michael Smirlock and William Marshall ("An Examination of the Empirical Relationship Between the Dividend and Investment Decisions," *Journal of Finance* 38 [1983]: 1659–67).

7. Kose John and Joseph Williams, "Dividends, Dilution, and Taxes: A Signaling Equilibrium," *Journal of Finance* 40 (1985): 1053–70. Merton Miller and Kevin Rock, "Dividend Policy Under Asymmetric Information," *Journal of Finance* 40 (1985): 1031–51.

8. DeAngelo and Masulis also considered some analytical issues associated with the independence of dividend and financing decisions and the conditions necessary for both decisions to leave the firm's market value invariant. See Harry DeAngelo and Ronald W. Masulis, "Leverage and Dividend Irrelevance under Corporate and Personal Taxation," *Journal of Finance* 35 (1980): 453–64.

9. Avner Kalay and Adam Shimrat, "On the Payment of Equity Financed Dividends," New York University Working Paper, 1986.

Chapter 11: Summary of the Evidence and Suggested Avenues of Future Research

1. Michael C. Jensen and William H. Meckling, "Theory of the Firm: Managerial Behavior, Agency Costs and Ownership Structure," *Journal of Financial Economics 3* (1976): 305–60. Stewart Myers and Nicholas Majluf, "Corporate Financing and Investment Decisions When Firms Have Information Investors Do Not Have," *Journal of Financial Economics 13* (1984): 187–221.

Names Index

Subject Index

About the Author

Ronald W. Masulis is the James M. Collins Professor of Finance
and an adjunct professor in the Department of Economics at
Southern Methodist University. Previously he taught in the
Graduate School of Management, UCLA, and served as finan-
cial economist with several government agencies, including the
Securities and Exchange Commission, the Federal Home Loan
Bank Board, and the Federal Savings and Loan Insurance Cor-
poration. He received his M.B.A. and Ph.D. from the Graduate
School of Business, University of Chicago.

Dr. Masulis serves on the Board of Directors of the American
Finance Association, the Executive Committee of the Western
Finance Association and is associate editor of the *Journal of Finance,
Journal of Financial Economics, Review of Financial Studies*, and *Jour-
nal of Financial and Quantitative Analysis*. He is also a grant reviewer
for the National Science Foundation and the Research Council of
Canada. His work in corporate finance and financial institutions
is widely cited.

DATE DUE

GAYLORD			PRINTED IN U.S.A.